"From Beginning to Last"

The Art of Making Beautiful Fashion Doll Shoes

By

Timothy J. Alberts & M. Dalton King

With

Pat Henry

Additional copies of this book may be purchased at $24.95 plus postage from

Hobby House Press, Inc.
1 Corporate Drive
Grantsville, MD 21536
1-800-554-1447
www.hobbyhouse.com
or from your favorite bookstore or dealer.

Published by Hobby House Press, Inc.
Grantsville, MD 21536

Printed in the United States of America

ISBN: 0-87588-561-6

Table of Contents

Introduction

I began developing my techniques for making shoes in the early 1990s, when I was creating my doll Chloe, and participating in the beginnings of the Gene project.

Chloe is a doll that is dressed in the height of 18th century fashion. Since I was designing the clothes, buying fabrics, and looking for accessories, it became very clear to me that I wouldn't be able to find shoes to equal the quality of the outfits I was making. The obvious solution was to make my own. But that meant figuring out how to make shoes using methods that could be implemented in the home rather than in a factory and at the same time give me the look I so desired for my shoes.

To that end I researched how shoes are actually made and adapted the big foot methods for miniature feet. Along the way I developed techniques of my own, such as the use of alginate to make molds, and a way to make the tiny heels I needed for smaller footed dolls such as Gene.

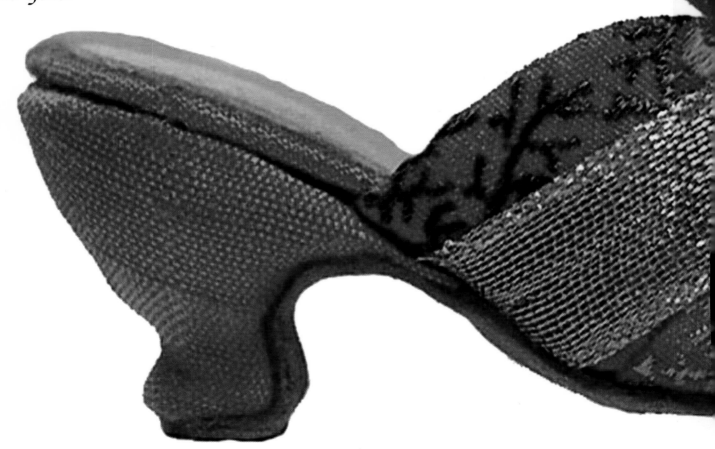

I hadn't given any thought to making my techniques public until I went to the first Gene convention and put three dolls, "Crème de Cassis," "Capri" (now known as "Incognito"), and "Summertime" up for auction. People saw the shoes I had made for "Summertime," as well as those I had done for Doug James' "USO" entry, and began to ask me for directions on how to make similar shoes for their dolls.

The response was the same at the second convention when I displayed my entries, "Countess Bewitched" and "Dawn's Ghost." People really wanted to know how to make those shoes. Thoroughly convinced now that there was an interest in, and a market for, my methods, I decided to do a video. I was working on putting the video together when my friend Sonia Rivera, publisher of the Fashion Doll Scene, suggested I also write a book. This book is the result of her suggestion.

It will take you through all the steps required to make beautiful doll shoes, starting first with lasts, after that, heels, and then the actual shoes themselves, with demonstrations on how to make both fabric and leather shoes. Along the way, we've included lots of pictures of the shoes I've made over the years and some of the lovely dolls that are now wearing those shoes.

You will, simply by following my techniques, be able to produce shoes that are works of art in themselves. The days of shoes being the least thought about accessory are over. So let's begin what I believe can only be a successful collaboration, with chapter one and a description of the parts of shoe.

Desiree, a unique 18th Century porcelain doll with molded hair.
Tim designed both the gown and the shoes for this doll.
Collection of Timothy J. Alberts.

Chapter 1

If The Shoe Fits…

And that is the problem isn't it? So often the shoe doesn't fit when they are made for a doll. They fall off, or worse yet, come apart in your hand as you are trying to force them onto your doll's feet. It's a much too common sight, seeing a doll falling off her heels, or seeing those same heels hanging from the ankles, held to the foot only by the grace of a flimsy ribbon. And that, to our minds, isn't even the least of it. How many times have you purchased a beautiful doll only to realize that the shoes come nowhere close to matching the excellence of its outfit? Far too often is the answer from far too many.

The solution? Doll companies, to their credit, are slowly beginning to realize the importance of shoes and that nothing finishes an outfit quite so completely as a well-shod foot. But their efforts are still determined by the bottom line and not likely to win real accolades any time soon. For the making of a shoe, a really good shoe, whether it be for a human or a doll, is an intricate matter, not difficult, but time consuming. The real solution is to either buy your doll shoes from someone who makes custom pairs, or make them yourself! That is where we come in.

This book is about making doll shoes, lovely, beautiful shoes that glide onto your doll's feet. Starting with this chapter, and continuing with the ones that follow, we will teach you how to make doll shoes, step by step. Shoes like the ones featured on the pages of this book.

We will begin by guiding you through the process of making lasts, the solid foundation upon which all shoes are made, and follow that by teaching you how to make heels. We will then show you how to actually make the shoes, demonstrating with a pair made from fabric and one made from leather. We end the book with a chapter called "Finishing Touches," a chapter with ideas on how to add just a touch more élan to the finished product, your custom made shoes.

But before we can talk about the finished product you first must make the shoes, and there is no better place to start than with a brief description of each of the parts of a shoe. You'll find this information necessary, for the terms used to describe the parts of a shoe are used over and over again in this book.

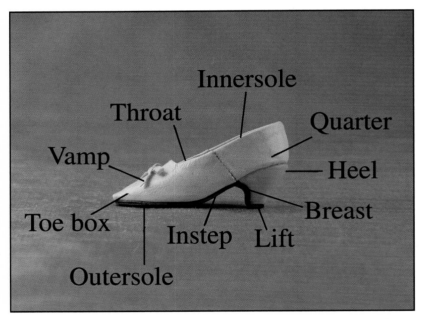

A diagram of a classically shaped shoe with all the parts named.

The throat, is the top line of the shoe, that which starts at the vamp and fits around the foot.

The vamp of the shoe covers the arch section of the foot. In period or sporty type shoes, the vamp is where the tongue of the shoe is situated.

The toe box, at the front of the shoe, is, where the toes fit. The size and shape of the toe box is determined by a combination of the size and shape of the toes and the fashion toe extension. The shape of the toe box is generally one of three basic shapes, round, square or pointed, the choice of which is usually determined by the fashion dictates of the day. And, just as with real shoes, the toe box should fit comfortably over the front section of the foot.

Comfort isn't an issue with miniature shoes for your doll isn't likely to complain if the shoes pinch but you do want a smooth fit just for the look of it.

The quarter is located at the back part of the shoe and fits the sides of the heel. A good fit here is important in keeping the shoe on the foot.

The heel is the bottom-back section of the shoe and provides both support and height. The shape and height of the heel is, just like the toe box, determined by what is considered fashionable, whether it be a Louis heel or a spike.

The breast is the forward-front section of the heel, located directly beneath where the instep meets the heel.

The lift is the bottom-most section of the heel. It serves a dual purpose, for while it finishes off the heel it also protects the heel from direct contact with the ground.

The instep is the bottom of the arch.

The innersole is the inner part of the shoe upon which the foot rests.

The sole or outer-sole is the bottom of the shoe.

You are ready now, to start making doll shoes. We assure you, it's easier than it may, at first, appear. But to ensure better success, we have a few suggestions. First, read each chapter through thoroughly, familiarize yourself with the techniques and materials used in each of them. Some of the materials used may seem strange, but don't worry, there is a source guide in the back of the book which will define the materials and tell you where to get them. Secondly, take your time, there is no need to rush, mastery of these techniques is not difficult to attain, and when working in miniature, accuracy is of the utmost importance. Finally, relax, enjoy the process, it is now only a matter of time before your doll will have new shoes for her feet.

So, let's begin, with the last!

*A 17th Century shoe, designed by Timothy, featuring a red heel,
which was so evocative of court dress at the time.*

Chapter 2

<u>The Molded Last</u>

To make a shoe, any shoe, whether it be for a human foot or a doll's, you will need a last, so that is where we will begin, with the last.

The last is the solid shape upon which a shoe is built. That shape is an exact replica of the foot, to which a fashion toe extension has been added. The fashion toe extension begins at the place on the foot where the toes bend and extend forward to what would be the tip of the shoe. Its shape is determined by the fashion of the day. Thus it is that the fashion toe, along with the heel, greatly influences the style of a shoe and gives it a definitive look of a particular period in time. For example, in the 1660s, the toes on shoes were rounded, giving the foot a very solid, secure look, while in the 1960s the toe was pointed, which produced a much sleeker, sharper profile to the foot.

Beyond making a fashion statement, the toe extension provides two additional benefits. It elongates the foot and gives a more graceful slide to the shoe while at the same time adding balance and strength to the structure of the shoe.

Doll affixed in the flight position.

The doll's leg is immersed in the alginate. Hold other leg while setting.

Carefully remove the doll's leg from the mold. Mold is ready for plaster slurry.

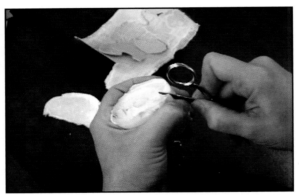

Using a knife or scissors to carefully remove the plaster last from the alginate.

Drawing the toe pattern, to which the fashion toe extension will be added.

The toe pattern with a 1950s style toe pattern added.

For commercial purposes, lasts are generally made from either wood or some type of metal. While we do give instructions for making a wooden last in chapter 3, there is an alternative method which can be used, one which is particularly suited to dolls with small feet or those whose feet have been specifically made to wear high heels.

The molded last, which is the first of the two techniques for making lasts we are presenting in this book, is a method which involves making a negative mold of your doll's foot, creating a plaster positive of the foot itself, and then adding the fashion toe extension. To begin you will need the following materials.

Materials Needed

- Alginate
- Casting plaster
- Air hardening clay or paper clay
- Stiff white paper
- A pencil or Sharpie
- Disposable art scalpels or matte knife
- Fine sand paper
- Waxed paper cups (both 3 & 9 ounce)
- A spoon
- A stirring apparatus
- A mixing bowl or vessel
- Water
- Your doll
- An adjustable doll stand which is slightly larger than the one which normally fits

- Before you start, make sure the leg you are going to take the mold from is clean and dry. Also, remove any clothing from the doll's body that may get in the way or become soiled.
- Affix your doll to the stand, arranging it in a flight position, extending one leg backward. It is the leg which is not extended that you will use to make the mold.

The pattern for the fashion toe extension, glued to the plaster last.

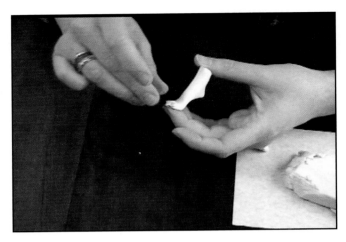

Using your paper pattern as a guide, use clay to mold the fashion toe extension onto the plaster last.

The toe extension is dry, and the plaster last has been sanded to give it a smooth finish. You are now ready to begin making shoes!

- *Slide the doll's body up the stand just enough so that you can lower the straight leg into an empty 9-ounce cup. This is a rehearsal of the positioning you will do when the alginate is in the cup. There should be empty space all around and beneath the foot of the doll. It is crucial that the doll's foot does not touch the bottom of the cup. Remove the cup from the doll's foot.*
- *Mix alginate and water, using the amounts suggested by the manufacturer, to create a slurry which has the consistency of a pancake batter (pourable). If yours is too thick, add more water, a small amount at a time. You'll find, though some manufacturers suggest otherwise, that cold water works best. And, because alginate sets up quickly, you'll want to work at a reasonably fast pace.*
- *Pour the slurry into the paper cup. Make sure you have mixed enough of the slurry to ensure that once you have poured it into the paper cup, the depth is deep enough to cover the leg up past the anklebone.*
- *Rotate the cup in your hand as you gently tap the bottom to bring bubbles to the top.*
- *Plunge your doll's foot into the center of the cup and hold the leg that is not in the alginate, steady, until the alginate begins to set.*
- *When the alginate has set, it will have acquired the consistency of a boiled egg white.*
- *Remove the leg from the "hardened" alginate by first wiggling it gently to loosen the grip of the mold. You will feel it release. Pull the leg out of the mold, heel first if possible.*
- *The hole that is left in the alginate is your negative mold.*
- *Mix casting plaster and water according to the directions on the box. The mixture should be on the thin side to facilitate it flowing into all the hollows of the mold.*
- *Spoon the plaster into the hole in the alginate, filling it to the top of the mold.*
- *Rotate the cup in you hand as you tap the bottom to release bubbles.*
- *Let the plaster dry completely.*
- *Once the plaster has "cured," tear away the paper cup.*
- *Using a matte knife, make a cut down the side of the alginate. Insert your thumbs and break the alginate open, thus releasing the plaster last inside.*

- With a matte knife or disposable scalpel, clean up any irregularities.
- Allow the plaster last to dry completely.
- To make the fashion toe extension, lay the last on a piece of cardstock and using the pencil or Sharpie mark around the toes, starting and ending at the bend point of the toes.
- On your pattern, starting at the big toe, sketch the desired toe shape.
- Cut out the paper pattern and using a dab of glue, attach it to the plaster last, attaching it at the point where the toes bend. Make sure the toes match your original trace line. Trim off any excess necessary to fit the shape of the foot.
- Using the paper pattern as your guide, mold paper clay onto the toe point, working the clay until you are satisfied with the shape. Remember that the toe box has to be at least as high as the big toe.
- Let the clay dry.
- Peel off the paper pattern from the bottom of the toes, and use the sandpaper to remove any traces of the glue that might remain.
- Give the last a light sanding overall to smooth any rough edges and refine its shape, as well.
- Keep in mind that if your doll has a definite left and right foot, you will have to make a last for each foot. And when you make the paper pattern for the toe extension, you will have to flip it to accommodate the opposite foot.

Hints & Tips

When purchasing alginate, be sure not to buy the fast setting type. Regular alginate sets up quickly enough, and using the fast set variety places you at a disadvantage.

When mixing the slurry, make sure you mix enough to accommodate your needs, for you won't have time to mix a second batch before the first one sets. It is better to have too much rather than too little.

Take care not to jiggle the feet as the alginate is setting up.

When you are removing the leg from the mold, you may find that the heel tears a bit of the top of it. Don't worry, that won't affect the successful outcome of your last.

Alginate doesn't have a long shelf life and will start to shrink as soon as it begins to dry, so it would be best not to let mold sit for too long before pouring in the plaster.

If the doll has a definite right and left foot, you will have to make a mold for each foot. We would suggest making both alginate molds first, and then mix up enough plaster to pour into both at the same time. After the plaster lasts have cured completely, use a pencil to mark the top of each, appropriately, with either an L or an R.

When making the pattern for the toe extension, the extension should come off the big toe, and veer to the left or the right, depending on which foot you are doing, rather than being centered.

Remember to flip the pattern for the toe extension if you are doing a right and left foot.

If your paper clay has dried you can knead it with a little water to soften it.

Most modern shoes are made with the toe extension coming from the big toe, period shoes were more centered, with the toe shape placed in the middle of the foot.

For each different toe shape, pointed, square, or round, you will have to make a separate last.

Once it is dry, you can peel the remaining alginate from the bowl.

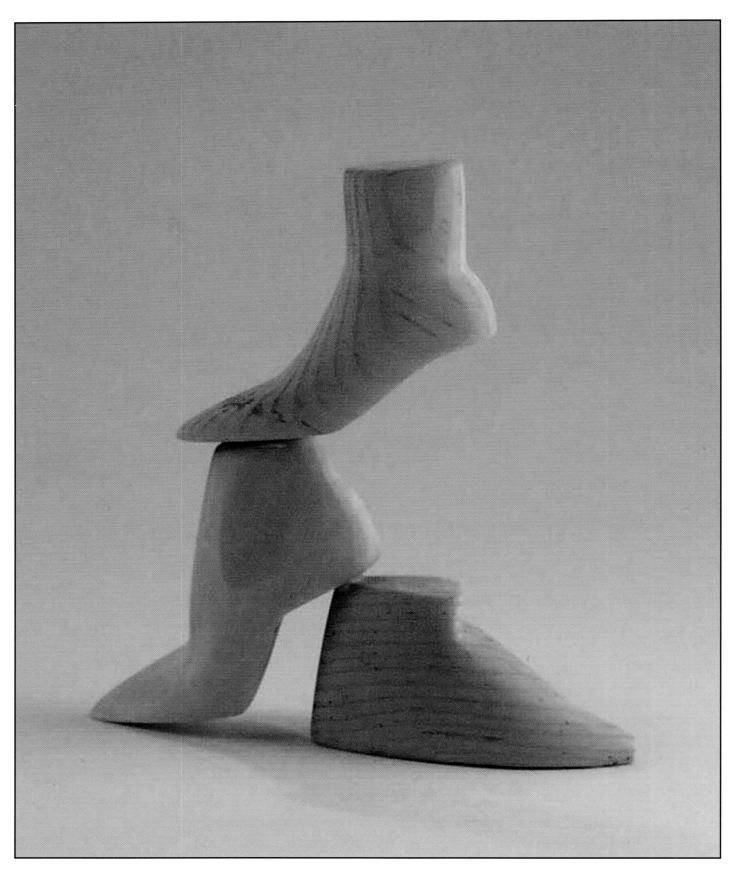

Carved wooden lasts made for different dolls' feet.

Chapter 3

The Carved Last

Carving the last is an excellent alternative to molding the last. It is often easier when working with larger sized dolls, such as Madame Alexander's Cissy, to carve the last, for the size of larger dolls may be an encumbrance when trying to mold a last. Another plus is, once you have carved a last, it can be used forever and you can make as many pairs of shoes as you wish for as long as you want. Bear in mind, that for each different shaped toe (round, pointed, or square) you will have to carve a separate last.

There is another factor to consider when working with larger-sized dolls, and that is the matter of the universal last. A universal last is one that will accommodate both feet of your doll, where there is no real, discernible difference between the two. "Simple feet" are quite a common occurrence on larger dolls and means that you would only have to carve one last, whereas, with most smaller dolls you will find that they have a definite left and right foot and therefore require two separate and distinct lasts.

19

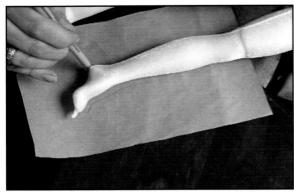

Tracing the profile of the doll's leg on brown craft paper.

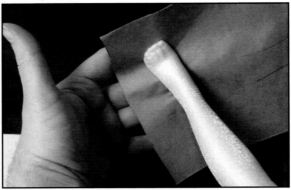

Making a paper pattern of the sole, using the doll's foot.

An example of a completed sole tracing.

The fashion toe extension has been added to both the leg profile and the sole pattern.

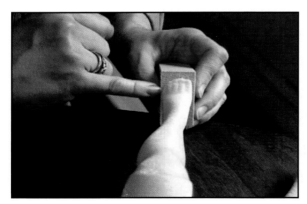

Make sure your block of wood is wide enough to accomodate the foot.

The profile traced onto the block of wood.

In this chapter, because we are using a larger doll to demonstrate how to carve a last, the last which has been produced is a universal one. If you should choose to carve a last for a doll that has smaller feet, or one with feet which have been specifically designed for high heels, you will have to carve a last for each foot. The process is the same, whether the foot you are carving the last for is large or small.

There is one final thing we would like to say before we begin explaining how to carve a last for your doll and that is, don't be afraid of the procedure! We admit it does begin to sound and look intimidating when there is talk of jig and band saws. But we believe you'll find that if you just follow the process step by step, and, if necessary, employ the help of a friend, neighbor, or family member, you'll find it easier than you first may have imagined. Take a deep breath and let's begin with the materials you'll need.

Materials needed:

- Stiff white paper
- Cardstock
- A pencil (preferably a mechanical one) or Sharpie®
- Scissors
- A piece of white pine or bass which is no more than ¼-inch wider than the total • Width of your doll's foot
- Various grades of sandpaper
- Calipers
- A dremel with the drum sander attachment
- The use of a band or jig saw
- Your doll

• Make a profile tracing of the doll's leg by laying the leg down, sideways, on the paper. Using the pencil, trace the outline of the foot and part of the leg. You'll find that for larger dolls you don't need to go very high up the leg but for smaller dolls you may want to trace as high as the calf or knee. This extra length will give you room to maneuver with, and something to hold onto when making the shoe.

The wooden profile being cut out on a band saw.

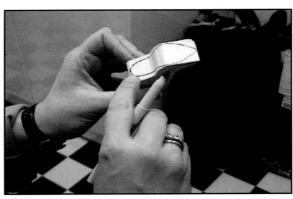

Draw the sole pattern on the bottom of the foot.

The front of the toe being cut out on the band saw.

The toe portion of the last, after being cut.

Now the heel section is ready to be trimmed away on the band saw.

Using the Dremel to refine the shape of the developing wooden last.

This is not a factor with larger lasts, for their sheer size alone makes them easier to work with.

• Lay the foot you are making the last for, sole down, on the paper and draw the outline of the foot, moving the pencil around the heel, instep and foot.

• Cut your paper patterns out and transfer them to cardstock. Remember, if you are doing lasts for a definite right and left foot, the sole pattern will have to be flipped to accommodate the variation in the toe shape that opposite feet have.

• Draw the fashion toe extension of your choice (square, round, or pointed) onto both the leg profile and sole cardstock patterns. There are a few guidelines to keep in mind when drawing the toe extension. If you are drawing the toe extension onto what is going to be a universal last, you will want the toe extension to come off the middle of the foot, thus accommodating both feet with a single last. For a definite and right and left foot, the toe extension should come off the big toe, left toe for the left shoe, right toe for right shoe.

• Cut out the cardstock patterns

• Before tracing the cardstock patterns onto your block of wood, make sure the piece of wood is big enough to accommodate the doll's foot, without being too big. You can gauge the size of the wood by laying the doll's foot against the narrow side of the wood. The piece should be no less than ¼-inch plus the size of your doll's foot.

• Using a Sharpie, trace the leg profile onto the block of wood.

• The next step will be to cut the leg profile out of the wood. Be sure to take the sole pattern with you when you go to cut out the wood.

• To begin to cut the profile out of the wood, first draw a series of relief cuts, perpendicular to the pattern, at each curve point, on the wooden profile. These relief cuts will make it easier for the saw blade to negotiate the curves and sharp points of the profile.

• Using a band saw, cut through the drawn lines, from the outside edge of the wood right up to the outside edge of the pattern.

• Cut the profile of the leg out of the wood.

• Once the profile has been cut, lay the sole pattern on the bottom of the wooden foot, matching the toe and heel points against the edges of the wood.

Check the size of your toe box with calipers to make sure the last is the same size as your dolls' foot.

As stated in the instructions, you should check the last in several areas.

Remember when making a universal last, the sole should have a neutral shape.

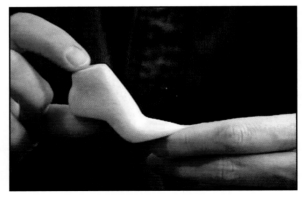

The completely finished carved last.

- *Use a Sharpie®, pen, or pencil, to trace the sole pattern onto the bottom of the foot.*
- *Using the saw, cut off whatever extra wood is necessary to match the shape of the sole.*
- *Place the sole pattern on top of the wooden profile and trace the toe point, making sure the toe point of the pattern matches the edge of the wood.*
- *Once again draw relief cuts, around the shape of the toe, to facilitate the removal of the wood, then cut the toe shape out of the wood.*
- *Now that you have the "rough" cut of the last, you can begin to remove the excess wood and refine its shape by using the Dremel drum sander, or sanding it manually, starting with a medium grade sandpaper.*
- *As you sand the last to its finished shape, keep checking the size and shape of your last by measuring it with a pair of calipers against the foot you are replicating. The points to check are the high point of the foot (the arch), the width of the foot (from side to side), the height of the toes (for you want to be sure the toe box will be high enough to actually fit over the toes), and the top of the foot, just beneath the ankle.*
- *When the last is nearly finished, use a fine grade sandpaper to give it a "polished look."*
- *If you wish, you can polyurethane the last. It is not at all necessary but will give your last a "prettier" look if you wish. But be sure the polyurethane is completely dry before beginning to make shoes.*

Tips & Hints

Always wear safety glasses when working with power tools such as band saws.

A 10-inch circular band saw with ¼-inch blade was used to cut out the lasts in this book.

Cutting off the excess wood from around the toe and sole makes finishing the last, and any handwork that must be done, a great deal easier, and faster.

Each new toe shape (round, square, pointed) requires a new last.

When tracing the leg profile onto the wood. Keep in mind that it helps, when working with smaller dolls, if the leg extension goes up to the knee or calf, for it gives you something to hold onto when making the shoe.

Mechanical pencils are very handy when tracing the leg profile and the sole, for by laying the pencil against the leg or foot and then tracing, the actual tracing turns out to be slightly larger than the patterns themselves, which gives you a little extra space to play with.

It would be best to make your tracings as accurate as possible, any extra space needed has already been worked into the instructions.

Remember, when drawing the toe extension, that you must make sure that the extension is wide enough to accommodate the width of the toes.

When sketching the toe extension try for graceful curving lines, for you want that reflected in your shoe rather then lines which appear too long, or worse yet, stumpy.

Don't be concerned if you don't have a Dremel, the wood is soft enough to be finished by hand, it will just take a little longer, though hand finishing will give you the advantage of being able to control the shape better.

Because the wood used for these lasts is so soft you could, if you are so inclined, carve the entire last by hand.

When finishing a universal last, and you get to the stage where you are sanding and using the calipers, another good measurement to check would be across the bottom of the sole, from the point where the toes break, all the way up to the instep. Make sure that both sides are as close to being exactly the same shape as possible.

The original "Night At Versailles", designed by Timothy J. Alberts.

Chapter 4

Heels

Now that you have your last, you need a heel. The heel is the bottom-back portion of the shoe and provides both height and support. In the case of dolls, the shape of the heel will be determined by the style of shoe you are making. If it is a period shoe, research will provide you with the styles fashionable at the time, for a modern shoe, you only need to look in fashion magazines or shoe stores.

It is also important, when choosing the shape of your heel, to consider its appropriateness for the shoe you are making. How will the heel look when attached to the base of the shoe? Does it blend with the chosen style or does it seem to be at odds with the overall look that you are aiming to achieve? For example, sharp stiletto heels wouldn't ordinarily work on shoes that have the shape and decoration evocative of the French court shoe because the two would, stylistically, seem to be in opposition to, or clash with each other. Consequently, there would be no flow to your shoe, the base and heel would not to be "of a piece."

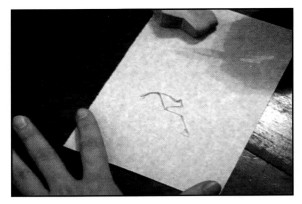

The first thing to do is to make a sketch of the type of heel desired.

Place the clay directly on the heel of the last.

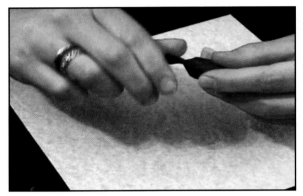

Using your fingers, begin sculpting.

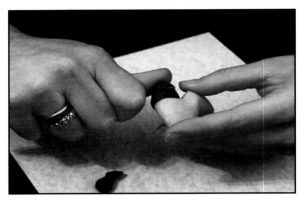

Continue sculpting, using any tools you may have to carve the heel.

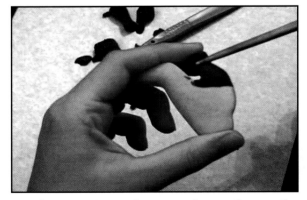

Refine your sculpt until you have the desired shape.

The sculpted heel ready for the next step.

For example, for the purposes of this book, one of the dolls we demonstrate making shoes for is the Madame Alexander Cissy bridal doll. Because that doll is dressed formally, in a wedding gown, the shoe being made is of a classical style, long, sleek vamp, and pointed toe. The heel that we feel would best compliment this shoe is in fact the elegant court, or Louis, heel. It too has classical lines, and suits the overall formal appeal of the shoe. An additional benefit to the use of the Louis heel is that because it extends way under the shoe it supports the foot and holds the doll's weight well.

Louis heel or not, whatever heel you do choose to make, the techniques demonstrated in this chapter will work to fulfill your need. Likewise, the materials needed remain the same.

Materials needed:

- Drawing paper
- A pencil or Sharpie®
- Sulphur-free clay
- A single edged razor blade
- Cheesecloth
- Petroleum jelly
- Liquid rubber latex
- Plaster of Paris
- Sculpting tools such as a disposable scalpel and thin wooden dowels (optional)
- The lid of a small jewelry box or a cut down milk carton
- Several small paintbrushes
- Durham's water putty
- Sobo glue
- Fine grade sandpaper
- 3 & 9-ounce paper cups
- A few long straight pins with a beaded head
- A spoon or stirrer
- Water

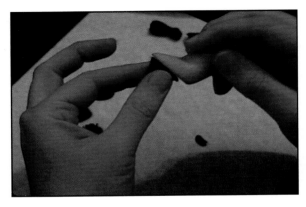

Use the last to smooth the top of the clay heel.

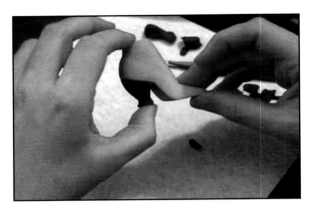

Place the sculpted heel on the last to check size and shape.

Using a single-edged razor, cut the heel exactly in half.

Place the dissected heel on the last, to check that its' shape hasn't become distorted.

The heel halves have been coated with petroleum jelly, and are waiting for the first coat of liquid latex.

Applying the first coat of the liquid latex.

- Begin by drawing a sketch of the shape of heel desired. This will be your reference as you make your heel.
- Soften the clay by working it with your fingers. In its natural state sulfur-free clay is very stiff, and the warmth from your hands as well as the oils from your skin will help soften it.
- Using your sketch as a guide, sculpt the heel directly onto the last. Work the clay until you have a shape you are satisfied with. As you are sculpting you can use the tools such as the scalpel to cut excess clay away, or the dowels to smooth the curves and round the edges.
- Carefully remove the heel from the last.
- Use the flat edge of the last to smooth the top of the clay heel.
- Lightly position the heel on the last for one final check on its size and shape. Check, also, the heel's orientation on the last.
- Refrigerate the heel for an hour or until it becomes very firm.
- Remove the heel from the fridge, and place it, breast side down on a flat surface. Using the single-edged razor blade cut the heel into two equal halves.
- Lightly put the heel halves together and place them on the last to make sure the cutting hasn't distorted the shape.
- Remove the heel from the last and separate the halves.
- Begin to make the mold by placing the heel halves, flat side down, in the center of the box top, leaving a space between the two halves.
- Using a paintbrush, lightly coat the halves, the bottom and sides of the box with a thin layer of petroleum jelly.
- Use a clean brush to coat the halves and the bottom surface of the box, only, with a very thin layer of liquid rubber latex. Break any bubbles, which may appear, with the hairs of the brush.
- Let the latex dry completely. When you first paint on the latex, you will notice that it is white in color, as it cures (dries) it will turn to a tan color. You can also test dryness by touching it. There will be no sign of "tackiness" when the latex is dry.
- Apply a second coat of the latex in the same way you did the first and let it dry completely.

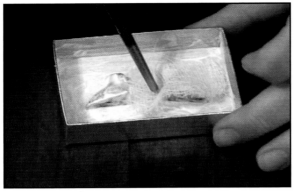

Applying a thick layer of latex to the cheesecloth.

Pouring the plaster.

Peel the box away to free your mold.

Take the rubber mold off the plaster mother, and pop out the clay heels.

Replace the rubber mold onto the plaster mother.

Pour the slurry of water putty into the heel mold.

- *Apply a third coat and let it dry.*
- *Cut the cheesecloth into small pieces (this allows for greater mobility).*
- *Paint a thick layer of the latex over the halves.*
- *Lay a single layer of cheesecloth over the halves, and the bottom of the box. Press the cheesecloth into the sides and crevices of the halves, using the paintbrush tip to do so.*
- *Paint a thick layer of latex onto the cheesecloth, pressing into the edges of the heel halves as you do so. Let dry thoroughly.*
- *Add two additional, thick, layers of latex, letting each layer dry completely before adding the next.*
- *When the rubber is dried, mix a small amount of plaster of Paris and water according to package instructions. Pour the plaster of Paris over the rubber mold, filling the lid up completely. By doing this, you are making a mother mold. When dry, the plaster of Paris will cradle the latex mold and keep it from distorting when you are working with it.*
- *When the plaster of Paris is dry, peel away the box.*
- *Carefully lift the rubber mold off the plaster.*
- *Gently pop out the clay halves.*
- *Set the rubber mold back into the plaster mother mold.*
- *Begin making the heels by mixing enough water putty and water to give you a fairly thin slurry.*
- *Pour the slurry into the two molds, filling them to ¾ full.*
- *Using the beaded head of the pin, work the putty in each of the two halves, making sure the slurry gets into all the crevices. Break up any bubbles as you "stir" with the pin head.*
- *Finish filling up the molds.*
- *Let the halves dry completely.*
- *Remove the dried halves from the mold. Glue them together with the Sobo.*
- *If there are any cracks or holes, fill them with water putty and let them dry.*
- *Give the heel a light sanding to remove any rough edges or surface irregularities.*
- *Your first heel is ready to be covered, now make a second one.*

Working the water putty with the head of a pin to remove bubbles.

The finished heel ready to be covered with leather or fabric.

Hints & Tips

The *Louis*, or court, heel is sometimes called a wasted heel.

When drawing the sketch for your heel, follow the line of the heel from the last to give a more graceful curve to your heel. And, as you draw, try to approximate the size needed for your heel. Doing so will make it easier to make size adjustments and give you an excellent reference point when you begin to sculpt the clay on the last.

Try not to handle the chilled clay too much lest it warm to your touch, and soften, thereby possibly distorting the shape of the heel.

When coating the heel halves with the first three coats of liquid rubber latex, try to keep the coatings as thin as possible to ensure a crisper mold and a superior shape for your heel.

Using cheesecloth allows you to build a stronger mold, faster. The alternative to the cheesecloth would be even more layers of the latex.

Remember that the latex isn't completely dry if it hasn't turned a tan color and lost its tackiness.

An Alternative Method for Making A Heel

Shoe made from silver ribbon

As with everything in life there is always another way, an alternative method of accomplishing a desired end. So it is with heels.

This second method is quick, and most particularly suited for very small or tiny heels. The disadvantage is that as we are once again going to use alginate, the mold will have a short shelf life. You will only be able to get 3 or 4 heels, at the most, from the mold, and as before, when making the last you will have to work quickly. The materials needed to make this heel are, with the exception of the wood, the same ones required for the other techniques in this book.

Materials needed:

- A small piece of soft wood (less than a half inch)
- Alginate, water,
- Fine grade sandpaper
- A 3-ounce paper cup
- Several long straight pins with beaded heads.

The solid heel shape is placed into the alginate.

The alginate has set, and the cup has been cut down.

Loosening the heel from the alginate.

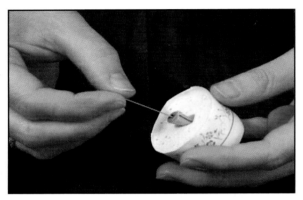

Pulling the heel from the alginate.

The empty mold is now ready for the slurry.

- The first step to making the alternative heel is to use a soft wood such as balsa and carve the shape you want. This should be relatively easy as you are working with such a small shape. Draw a sketch, as you did with the molded heel, and use that as a reference in achieving the desired shape.
- Before making the mold, check your carved heel against the last to ensure that the carved heel is of a correct, corresponding size.
- Once you are satisfied with the shape of your heel, and that it is the right size for the shoe you are making, attach the wide, flat end of your carved heel to a long straight pin with a bead on the end.
- Mix a slurry of alginate and water, the same consistency as you did for the molded last, and pour it into the paper cup and fill it half way up.
- Holding onto the beaded head of the pin, plunge the heel into the alginate, just up to the top of the heel. Keep holding the top of the pin until the alginate sets.
- Remove the carved heel from the alginate by first pressing down on the alginate, with your fingers, around the heel. This should loosen the alginate enough to allow you to just pull the heel out.
- Mix a slurry of water putty and water, as instructed in the first half of this chapter. Pour the water putty mix into your mold. Use the beaded end of a straight pin to stir the water putty in the mold, making sure the mix flows into all the crevices, and that all bubbles are broken.
- Let the heel dry.
- To release the heel from the mold, press down on the alginate surrounding the heel. The heel will pop up enough for you to be able to take it out.
- Fill any holes or cracks (if any) with water putty and let it dry.
- While the first heel is drying, pour a second one.
- Give the first heel a light sanding, if needed, to smooth and refine it.
- Finish the second heel.

Specially designed bridal shoes for Madame Alexander's Cissy doll.
The shoes are a delicate silk brocade.

Chapter 5

Fabric Shoes

Finally, now that all the technical bits are done, it's time to have some fun, and make some shoes. To begin, you'll have to ask yourself some questions and make some basic decisions. Are the shoes to be fabric or leather? If fabric, what material do you want to use, what color? Should the shoes be slings or pumps?

And then there is the matter of style. What style of gown or dress are you making the shoes for? Is it formal or daywear? Is it a period dress, or modern? The answers to these questions will determine what style shoe you want and whether a sling or a pump would be most appropriate.

As for the color of the shoe, do you wish to accent it with a similar tone or shade the color of the dress, or would you prefer to compliment it with a different color altogether? If there is any question of which color to choose, we suggest gathering swatches of the ones you have in mind and laying them next to the dress for comparison. You might even delay the decision for 24 hours, glancing at the

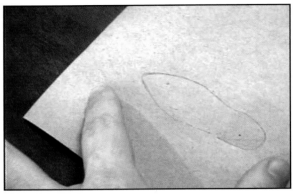

Tracing the sole pattern onto brown craft paper.

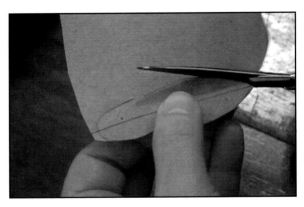

Cutting out the pattern, making sure both sides are equal.

The sole pattern with the line drawn down the center. Ready to begin making the innersole.

The acid free paper glued to the leather for the sole.

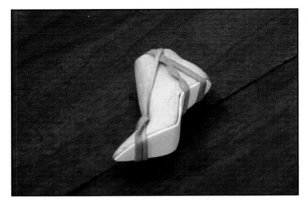

The innersole rubberbanded to the last.

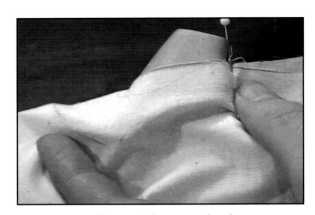

Draping the muslin on the last.

swatches from time to time, in differing intensities of light, day, dusk or evening. For the quality of light can make a difference in how a color strikes the eye, and a match which delights you in the evening could well horrify you come morning.

Finally, you must choose the fabric. It should be thin and tightly woven, or in other words strong but pliable. Silk and silk-wool blends, in our opinion, would be an ideal choice. For aside from the color range available in silk, silk is a joy to work with, since it is very easy to mold and shape. You'll especially appreciate silk's flexibility when you are wrapping fabric around a small little heel. Naturally, there are other fabrics which can be used, cotton being an excellent choice, and of course, there are ribbons.

Ribbons are a wonderful option when making miniature shoes. They are available in a wide range of fabrics, colors and designs, designs which, being small by nature, lend themselves easily to the ever-present problem of scale. And, ribbons have an additional advantage in the fact that you can buy them in small amounts, thus making them more cost effective than having to buy minimum yardage of fabrics.

So, you've made your choices as to fabric, color and style and are now itching to get your shoes started. We'll begin as we have in the previous chapters with a list of the supplies needed. Then, we'll take you through the process, step by step, of making your fabric shoes. (If you're making leather shoes, you find them detailed in chapter 6.)

Our model, (as we stated in chapter 4) and for demonstration purposes only, is Madame Alexander's Cissy bride doll. Cissy is dressed in a lovely wedding gown for which we decided to make a new pair of shoes. And, because her outfit is formal, we are going to make a pair of pumps, more specifically, a pair of court shoes with Louis heels. This style of the shoe, as well as the white silk brocade from which they are made, are a perfect match to the elegance of Cissy's outfit.

Keep in mind that Cissy doesn't have a definite right or left foot (as is so often the case with larger dolls), so you'll be working with a "universal" pattern as we explained in the chapter on wooden lasts (chapter 3). But before we get to that, let's go through the list of needed supplies first.

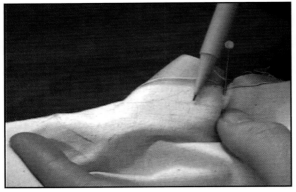

Make sure your grain line is going in the proper direction.

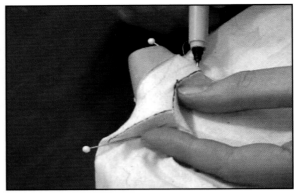

Marking the edge of the sole with a Sharpie®.

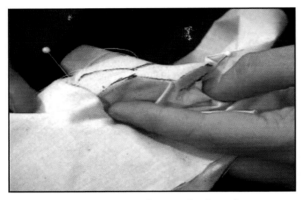

Marking the top line of the shoe.

This is your basic pattern.

The muslin has been "trued up", and is now ready to be traced on to brown craft paper.

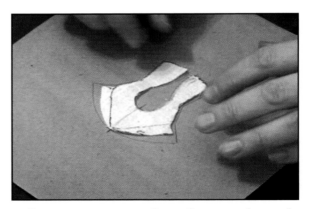

The pattern transferred to card stock.

Materials needed:

- *Fabric (for both the shoe and the interfacing) or ribbon*
- *A lightweight leather for the innersole, a medium gauge leather for the outer-sole*
- *A woven iron-on (fusible) interlining*
- *Brown craft paper*
- *Card stock*
- *A lightweight muslin*
- *Thin, acid free watercolor paper*
- *Assorted scissors*

- *An assortment of threads*
- *Sewing machine*
- *Iron*
- *A pencil or Sharpie*
- *Sobo glue*
- *Rubberbands*
- *Rulers (both curved and straightedged)*
- *An awl*
- *Pins, a padded surface*
- *A wet cloth for your hands*
- *Your last and heels*

- *Using your last, trace a pattern of the sole onto brown craft paper. To do so, hold the last against the brown craft paper and trace, as accurately as possible, and as close to the edge of the last as you can.*
- *Using a ruler, draw a line (lengthwise) down the center of the pattern. This line will be a reference point for you as you go along. Cut the paper pattern out. This pattern will serve for both the outer and innersole.*
- *Fold the sole pattern along the reference line. Be careful when folding because you want both sides (halves) to be exactly the same. If necessary, use the scissors to refine the shape or trim away any excess.*
- *Test the pattern against the sole of the foot, making sure that your sole pattern is the same exact shape as the sole of the last.*
- *Make the innersole by first tracing the sole pattern onto acid-free watercolor paper. Cut the pattern out.*
- *Check the innersole pattern against the bottom of your doll's foot for accuracy. Make adjustments or changes, as necessary.*
- *Glue the acid-free paper innersole onto the leather you have chosen for this purpose and cut it out. You'll find that a nice stiff, but thin, type of leather works best for the innersole. And, you will also find that the leather has a smooth side*

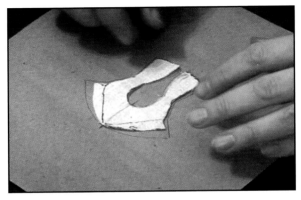

The original muslin laying on top of the card stock "upper" pattern.

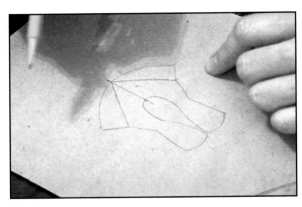

Draw a line connecting the dots.

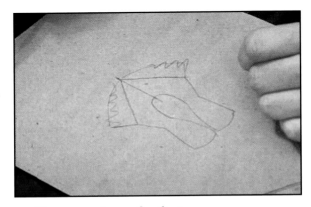

When cutting the lining pattern out, omit the section above the pricked line.

The lining pattern cut out and transferred to card stock.

This is the sole edge.

The muslin has been sewn along the stitch line.

and a rough, suede type side. You are going to glue the paper innersole to the rough side of the leather, which means that the smooth side of the leather is what is going to be touching your doll's foot when you place it in the finished shoe. Let the glue dry for a minute, or until it begins to set.

• Fit the innersole that you have just cut out onto the last and attach it with a rubber band. Leave the innersole on the last until it is dry. When it is completely dry remove the innersole from the last. You will see that it has taken on the shape of the last. Set it aside until you need it.

Now, before we continue with the instructions, we would like to take a moment to discuss grain. As with any project dealing with fabric (and ribbons, should that be the case), the grain line is very important. For how a fabric is cut will often make the difference between failure and success. The grain line of a fabric is determined by the threads which run horizontally and vertically in a fabric. The straight grain line runs parallel to the selvedge edge. The grain line which runs perpendicular to the selvedge line is called cross grain, but the cross grain line is seldom if ever used for anything, and certainly not here, in making shoes. Here, you will be only be concerned with the straight grain, and trying to make sure the fabric for your shoes are cut on such. The reason this is important is because you don't want to cut on the bias when making the "upper" section of your shoes. Cutting on the bias is when you cut diagonally on a fabric, thus introducing stretch and "give" into whatever you are making. And while cutting on the bias is a marvelous technique to use, you don't want to use it here, when making the basic shape for your shoes. To cut on the bias would cause the shoe shape to stretch, and that would give you major problems with stabilizing the shoe. (Bias will become a factor when you cover the heel, but you needn't pay any attention to that until later in this chapter.) For now, as we begin draping the muslin on the last, we are only concerned with the straight grain and how to keep the fabric on it.

• Begin making the muslin pattern for the upper part of the shoe by taking a piece of muslin, which is several times bigger than the size of your last, and cut a slit halfway across the muslin on the straight of the grain, which runs parallel to the selvedge edge. Using a ruler, draw a line from the point where the cut stops

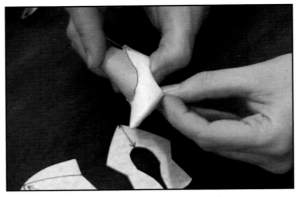

The muslin mock-up, now we almost have a shoe.

Determining the straight grain of the fabric.

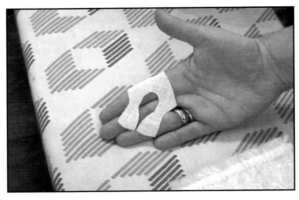

The interlining cut out.

The fusible, lightly touched with an iron.

Tracing the interfacing pattern onto the fabric.

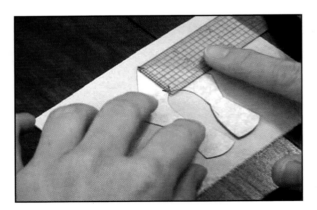

Again, determining the straight grain.

straight across the remaining half of the fabric. This will be a reference point for you.

• Slip your last into the slit, and pull the fabric so that it fits snugly but not too tightly on the last, right around to the back of the heel. It helps to pin the last at the back of the heel to hold the muslin in place. What you are going to do is pinch and pull the muslin until it fits the last perfectly. You can use pins if you need to. It is here where you need to be aware of the straight grain. Make sure the grain lines are as straight as they can be as the fit of the muslin extends back over the "quarter" of the last to the heel. Remember that the threads in the fabric should run parallel to the selvedge edge and the line we drew before placing the muslin on the last. As for positioning, the line we drew should remain in the center of the toe box, as you pull and pinch the fabric to fit.

• Once the fabric is fitted to the last, use a pencil or a Sharpie to mark the sole edge of the last. Do it on both sides of the last and up the center back at the heel. At the bottom of the foot (the sole), pull the fabric tightly and place a pin in the center of the sole. Draw a line along the pin you've just inserted, down the center of the sole. This will be your stitch line.

• It is at this point that the decision for a sling or a pump comes into play. Draw the top line of your shoe by sketching lines on the muslin that will encase the foot in a pump or that will slant upwards towards the back of the heel to make a sling. The height of the line you draw will determine how high up on the foot the shoe will end up being. Before you begin to draw your top line, make sure you know exactly how you want your shoe to look, and the orientation of your envisioned style to the last.

• Remove the muslin from the last, fold it in half along the straight grain line, refine (or true up) the lines and cut it out.

• Trace the pattern onto brown craft paper and true it up (refine all the edges). Use a ruler for the straight edges and curves for the rounded lines. Be sure to mark the straight grain line at the top of the pattern.

• Cut the pattern out. This is your upper shoe pattern.

• Transfer this pattern to cardstock for a more durable pattern. You'll be glad you did this when you have to trace this pattern onto the fabric, for the sturdiness of

The silk taffeta cut-out with the seam allowance.

The interfacing has been sewn onto the shoe fabric along the top line of the shoe.

Clipping the inside curve.

The silk taffeta has been turned to the inside and has been pressed flat.

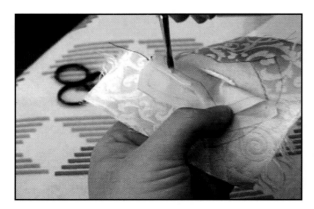

Gluing the interfacing to the fabric.

The stitch line at the toe of the shoe.

the card stock makes tracing so much easier. Be sure to mark the straight grain line for reference.

• Now we are going to make the lining (or inter-lining) pattern. Take the card stock pattern of the upper that you have just made, lay it on brown paper and trace it, (be sure to include the straight grain line). Lay the brown paper pattern on a padded surface (a folded towel will do) and lay your original muslin on the paper pattern, matching the lines where possible. Don't be thrown by how different the upper pattern is from the original, remember the upper pattern has been trued up.

• Using a sharp tool, such as an awl or needle, prick holes through the original sole line. Then using a pencil, draw a line that connects the dots that you have just pricked. Next, cut out the lining pattern, omitting any lines above the pricked line.

• Transfer the interlining pattern to cardstock.

• Place the interlining pattern on top of the shoe upper pattern, matching the straight grain lines. Using the upper pattern as your guide, mark the lining pattern with "sole edge" and "stitch line."

• It is at this point that, if you choose, you will make a muslin mock-up. You don't have to do this if you are confident about the fit of your patterns, but we have found that even though this step is time consuming, in the long run it is worth the time spent. For when you make the mock-up you will discover if there are any glitches, or refinements needed in your pattern, and you can make needed corrections without wasting any fabric.

The muslin mock-up:

To make your mock-up, cut the shoe, upper pattern from muslin. Make sure you cut it on the straight grain. Cut the interlining pattern from a woven, cotton fusible. Lay the interlining piece on the muslin, and touch briefly with a hot iron to secure it in place. Then place a press cloth over the interlining and press down for a few seconds or until the glue in the interlining has melted. (The press cloth is a great idea, because the glue sometimes seeps through and gets on your iron). Sew up the back of the muslin at the heel, and then sew under the sole on the stitch line. An additional help will be to stitch the top line of the mock-up in black thread, just so you will be able to see clearly how the top of the shoe will look on the foot.

51

Trimming the stitch line.

The heel section has been pinned together, and is ready to be sewn.

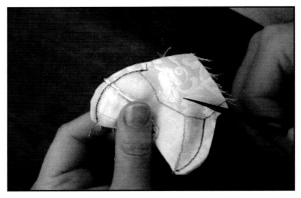

Trim away the excess fabric from the heel section which has just been sewn.

Turning the facing down.

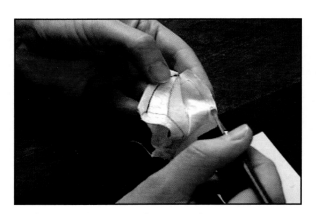

Gluing the interfacing down.

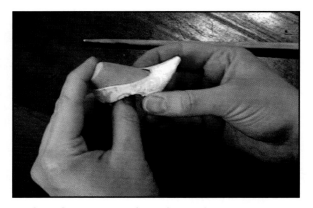

The shoe turned right side out.

After you have done the sewing, you'll be able to glimpse the beginnings of your shoe. Fit the mock-up on the last, making sure the foot of the last goes as far into the mock-up (just as it will in a shoe) as possible. You'll also want the mock-up to fit snugly at the back of the heel, and along the top line. If the fabric has stretched (as it sometimes will) and the mock-up is too big, pinch the excess fabric to see how much should be taken off your pattern. Then make the necessary correction(s) on your pattern. Your next step will be to begin making the shoe out of fabric.

• Lay a square of the fabric you wish to use, right side (the side of the fabric you want to be on the outside of your shoe) down on your work surface.

• Place the pattern for the shoe upper on the fabric. Be sure it is on the straight grain. To achieve this, use a ruler to measure from the selvedge edge to the grain line on your pattern. Make sure that the edge of the ruler lines up with your reference line. Do the same on the bottom of the pattern.

• Use a pencil to trace the outside edge of the pattern onto the fabric. It would be best if you use a mechanical pencil, trying not to press down too hard. You don't want the lines to show on the other side of the fabric. Also trace the inside (the top line of the shoe) line of the shoe.

• Take the interlining pattern piece and lay it inside the upper pattern lines you have just traced onto the fabric. Make sure the lines match, and then trace the top portion of the interlining pattern onto the fabric. This will be a reference that will let you know exactly where to place the iron-on before applying heat to it.

• The next step is to place the fusible (or iron-on interlining) on your work surface. The iron-on interlining (or fusible) is a woven cotton iron-on, which has been treated with glue on one side. The fusible should be placed with the glue side down. Lay the interlining pattern on the fusible. Pay attention to the straight of grain at both the top and bottom of the pattern. This should be easy for the grain lines will be very evident. Trace the pattern and cut the interlining out.

• Lay the interlining piece on the tracing of the upper on the fabric. Make sure the glue side is down and that the lines match. Touch the interlining lightly with a hot iron to secure it. Then cover the interlining with a press cloth and iron

Carefully slide the innersole and last into the shoe.

Gluing the excess fabric down.

Positioning the heel on the bias of the fabric.

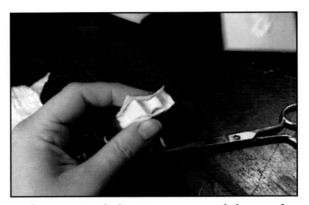

The excess fabric is trimmed from the heel.

Gluing the top of the heel down.

until the glue has melted. Let it cool. Do not cut this out, that step will come much later.

• The next step is to decide whether or not you want to do an interfacing for your shoe. Inter-facing means that the fabric you use will face the inside of the shoe, that is to say, your doll's foot will be right next to whatever fabric you choose. It's not always necessary, particularly when you have planned a relatively simple top-line to your shoe. In such cases you would clip the fabric, turn it down and glue it to the iron-on, not unlike the way the leather shoe is finished at the top-line (chapter 6). But because we're doing such an elegant shoe, made from a lovely fabric, we decided to make an interfacing to line the shoe, in this case with silk taffeta. The other advantage to using an interfacing is that it gives a very finished, clean look and retains the sharpness of the top line. So for the purposes of this chapter we are going to assume that you wouldn't dream of making a shoe that didn't have an interfacing, and we will proceed from there.

• Lay the interlining pattern on the interfacing fabric of your choice, making sure the grain lines match.. Trace the pattern onto the fabric. Take care to be accurate, especially when tracing the inside curve (the top line), and try to keep your pencil marks as light as possible so that they don't bleed through to the other side.

• Cut the interfacing out, leaving a small seam allowance on the outside edge (no less than ¼ inch) as you go. Do not cut the inside curved piece (the top line) out yet.

• Put the right sides of your fabrics (the shoe upper and the interfacing) together and pin them, making sure your pencil lines match up. Doing so will ensure that the interfacing is positioned directly on top of the fusible.

• Stitch along the top line (the inside curve) of your shoe, using a very small stitch (1-½).

• Carefully cut the center piece out. Because it is so narrow (particularly at the bottom) take care not to cut your sew line. When you have the curve cut out, clip lightly round it to facilitate turning.

• Turn the silk taffeta to the inside. You'll find it helps to give the seams a little finger press as you go.

The covered heel is ready to be glued onto the shoe.

Before gluing, be sure to check the orientation of the heel to the shoe itself.

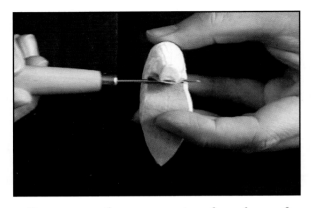

The innersole pattern is placed on the bottom of the shoe. It will be altered into the outersole pattern.

Adjusted outersole pattern and the outersole cut-out in leather.

Trim the outersole.

- Once the taffeta has been turned, press it in place. It's at this point, that if you want to do any decoration, like beading or embroidering the toe area, you should do it now while the shoe is still in a flat form. But be careful that any stitches you make only goes through the shoe fabric and the interlining (the fusible) but does not pierce the interfacing, thus preventing your stitches from showing on the inside of the shoe.

- The next step is to sew your shoe. Fold the shoe fabric in half, pull the interfacing out of your way at the front of the shoe, and pin through matching the pencil lines. Remember it is the stitch line you are pinning. Sew the stitch line at the toe using a small stitch. (1-½). When you get to the point, back stitch to knot the fabric.

- Trim the section you have just stitched and then make a small diagonal cut at the tip of the toe to facilitate turning. Be careful when trimming not to cut any of your sewn threads. Place a teeny dollop of glue at the toe (on the diagonal clip) to ensure the threads don't break. Let the glue dry.

- Next, pin the heel sections together. Make sure the stitch lines on both the shoe fabric and the interfacing match up. Stitch the heels, starting at the top with the interfacing portion of the heel and going straight through the shoe fabric portion of the heel. Use a slightly larger stitch than you have previously used (2).

- Trim the seam you have just sewn as well as cutting excess fabric away from the bottom of the shoe, below the sew line. Finger press the seams open.

- Turn the facing down.

- Glue the interfacing down by applying glue to the seam allowance edge of the silk taffeta, that we cut out. You should be able to see your pencil lines thus enabling you to match them as you press the fabric down. Do this all the way around the sole edge of the shoe. Let the glue partially dry.

- Give the seam allowance on the toe portion of your shoe a finger press and then turn the shape inside out. You'll need some type of blunt tipped tool to help you push the toe point out. Try the shoe shape out on your last, making sure the seam under the sole stays nice and flat. (If it bunches, it will show through the sole of the shoe when that is put on). Now this has been done before the glue is completely dry, so if you need to pull with your fingers to adjust the fit, you will be able to do so.

Making the pattern for the lift.

Gluing the lift.

The shoe is now ready to be decorated.

• *Steam press the "upper" of the shoe (on the last), to help keep the shape accurate. A press cloth will prevent the "upper" from being damaged from the iron or steam. The cloth is not necessary when you press the bottom of the shoe. As you steam and press the bottom, check to make sure that your original pencil lines are positioned on the edge of the last.*

• *Now, we are going to attach the upper shoe to the innersole. To do so, take the innersole you made earlier and hold it against the last (leather side touching the last, the acid free paper side up). Apply a small dab of glue to the outside toe portion of the innersole, then holding the innersole to the last, carefully slide the last into the toe of the shoe, then adjust the heel. Check your fit and make sure your sole seam is lying nice and flat against the innersole.*

• *Glue all excess fabric down, around the bottom of the sole. Let the "upper" dry to the innersole as you make the heel.*

• *The first thing we did was to paint our heel white. This isn't necessary if you* are using any fabric color but white. For some reason, the beige color of the Durham's bleeds through white, and after you gone through the process of making such a perfect shoe, it would be a shame to let such a small detail mar the look of the your shoe.

- To cover the heel, we are going to cut the fabric on the bias. The bias is at a 45 degree angle to the selvedge edge and the beauty of it is that bias has wonderful give and stretch, which gives it the ability to hug the shape of a heel. And that is exactly what you are going to need for your heel, because the heel is a round shape and you are going to wrap the fabric around it.

- Paint the heel lightly, with glue, all round (excluding the top, the breast of the heel and the lift).

- Take a small piece of your fabric and lay your heel on the bias. (Make sure that the side of the fabric showing on the outside of your heel is the same side that shows on the outside of the shoe).

- Start pulling the fabric snugly around the heel, pressing it into the wasted shape of the heel. Let the glue dry.

- Leaving no less than approximately ¼-inch all around, trim away the excess fabric. Keep in mind that on the breast you want the fabric to butt, not overlap, so check your fit as you go along.

- Paint a small amount of glue onto the breast of the heel and then press the fabric onto the breast, using your fingers to place it so that the ends meets directly in the center of the breast. Hold the fabric there until the glue begins to dry.

- Paint glue onto the top of the heel and press the excess fabric around the top into it, making it as smooth and tight as possible. Use a pointed tool if necessary to press and hold the fabric.

- Repeat this process of gluing and smoothing the excess fabric at the lift section of the heel.

- Now is the time to attach the heel to the shoe. Paint a small amount of the Sobo on the top of the heel you have just covered. You'll need to use enough glue to ensure that the heel is firmly attached, but not so much that the glue squeezes out onto the shoe. (Should the glue leak onto the shoe, use a pin or your fingernail to remove it from the cracks).

- Turn the shoe upside down and attach the heel. Check (by looking down the length of the shoe) the orientation of your placement, making sure your heel is on straight and that the heel is in a good position across the back of the shoe.
- Press the shoe and heel together with your fingers, and applying pressure, hold it in place until it dries.
- The next step is to make the pattern for your outer sole. To do this, first copy the innersole pattern onto brown craft paper and cut it out.
- Then take that tracing and lay it on the bottom of the shoe. Using a sharp tool, force the paper pattern down between the breast of the heel and the arch of the shoe.
- Draw an outline of the sole of the shoe by tracing along the outside edge of the shoe against the paper to make the pattern for the outer-sole. For some shoes you may find you have to extend the pattern to cover a longer length.
- Remove the brown paper pattern from the shoe and trim along the pencil lines you've just made. This will be your outer-sole pattern.
- Lay the adjusted pattern on a slightly thicker and less pliable leather, trace it and cut it out. Once again, the suede side is the one you are going to paint glue on. Be judicious with the amount of glue for you don't want it to squeeze out onto the shoe.
- Carefully lay the outer sole on the sole of the shoe. Adjust it, using whatever tools necessary, for the fit.
- Press the sole gently down between the breast of the heel and the arch. Make the sole as smooth as you can.
- Trim off any excess as necessary from the breast of the heel.
- Lay the shoe on your work surface. Press down on your shoe and roll the sole from side to side, to tamp down the leather, flatten and smooth it.
- When the glue has dried, trim any excess leather from the front of the shoe. For a more finished look, try to trim the front with a single cut of the scissors from each side.
- To make the lift, trace the bottom of the heel on brown paper and cut the pattern out. Once you have the pattern, cut it out of the same leather you used for the outer sole.

- Place glue on the suede side and lay it on the bottom of the heel. It should extend out just a tad from the fabric, just as a lift on a real shoe would. Trim any excess.

Congratulations! Your first shoe is now ready for decoration if you so desire. For suggestions see Chapter 7, "Finishing Touches."

- Make a second shoe to match the first.

Hints & Tips

Acid free watercolor paper is used for the innersole as a preventative measure. In most papers there is a chemical which, in time, will act to discolor and slowly deteriorate your fabric. Acid free paper does not have the same chemical make-up as regular paper and therefore will not harm your dolls when sustained contact is made.

Accuracy is of the utmost importance when working in miniature in general, and these shoes are no exception. The more careful you are to get the fit just right, the more successful the end result and the better pleased you will be.

It helps whenever you are working with glue to keep a dish with a wet cloth by your side. This makes it much easier to keep your fingers clean and eliminates smudges or stains getting on your fabric or leather.

Remember, if your doll has a definite right and left foot, you are going to have to flip the sole patterns when making the second shoe.

When ironing fusible, we use steam but it isn't necessary. An additional benefit to using a press cloth is that you can use a hotter iron than you might normally be able to.

Using Marking-Pencil Removal is an excellent way to remove unwanted pencil lines. (See the source guide.)

*"Little Mary", a Toni doll from the 1950s, is all done up for a party
down to her pink leather Mary Janes.
From the collection of M. Dalton King.*

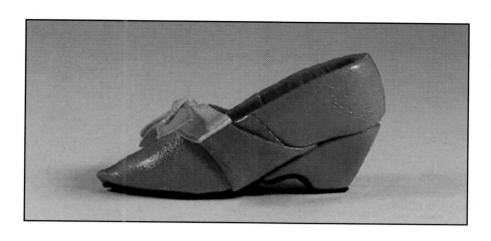

Chapter 6

Leather Shoes

At this point you've learned how to make lasts, heels, and fabric shoes. You are now

nearly an expert. There is only one more technique for you to master, and that is the making of leather shoes. The process is basically the same as the one used to make the fabric shoes. There are differences, however, and we will point them out as we once again take you through the shoemaking process, step by step.

The shoes we are making for this chapter are a pair of slings. Slings are an open-backed variation of the pump, and it is just this very variation that we want you to see. For making a sling will provide you with an opportunity to see just how you can take the basic pattern and adapt it to other styles and shapes. With the completion of these shoes, we feel you will have the basics down, and have acquired a good understanding of how to adapt the techniques to make any style shoe you wish.

Our model for this chapter is Ashton Drake's Gene. Gene is a perfect doll to use for this section for she is an excellent example of a doll whose feet are very small, she has a definite left and right foot, and her feet have been sculpted to wear high heels.

The sling back, drawn on the muslin.

The process for making the pattern for the leather shoes is the same as for the fabric shoes.

Applying glue to the clipped edge.

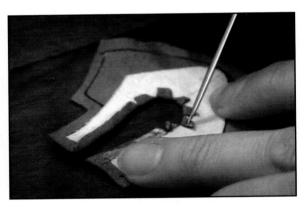

Turning the clipped curve back onto the cotton interlining.

Pressing the leather down with a dowel or similar tool.

Checking the leather for irregularities.

The shoes, demonstrated here, were made for a specific design, a copper colored, sheath, day dress and a Jaguar faux-fur coat. Because the coat and dress both have gold/russet tones, it was thought that brown shoes would suit the outfit best. Brown is a complimentary tone that will work well with either the coat or the dress worn separately or together as an ensemble. But the basic brown of the shoe has been jazzed up a bit by making the heels black. Using black for the heel adds a touch more panache to the style of the shoe and has an additional advantage in that the color of the heels will punch up the black markings of the coat. And while the clothes are 50's style, they are classic shapes which the sling, a classic shape in it's own right, will compliment without drawing too much attention away from the style of the clothes. These considerations of color and style are the very ones you can use to guide you when making your choices.

So let's begin this last step of your shoe seminar, with a list of the supplies needed.

Materials needed:

· Brown craft paper
· Card stock
· A lightweight muslin thin, acid free paper (for the shoes demonstrated in this chapter we use a black acid free paper, but depending on the color of your shoes you may choose white)
· Assorted scissors
· A paper or leather punch pencil
· A fine-point and ultra fine point Sharpie®
· Sobo® glue
· Rubberbands
· Rulers (both curved and straight edged)

· An awl
· Pins
· A padded surface (a towel will do)
· A tightly woven lightweight cotton
· A lightweight leather (preferably kid)
· A slightly thicker heavier weight leather (such as cow skin)
· Leather dye (optional)
· A leather finish or shoe wax
· A damp cloth to wipe your hands (thus preventing the glue from being transferred to your shoes)
· Your last and heels

The strap has been glued, notice how
the turned leather butts at the end.

Gluing the toe point.

Wrapping your leather "upper"
around the last.

Pulling the leather onto the innersole.

Burnishing the sole of the shoe
against a hard surface.

Gluing the arch.

• As we have said, the process for making the leather shoes is much the same as for the fabric shoes (chapter 5). You are going to drape the muslin on the last, pinching and pulling to achieve the shape of the shoe "upper."

• Using your Sharpie, outline the edge of the sole (also mark the stitch line as discussed in Chapter 5, for though you don't need a stitch line when making leather shoes, it will come in handy should you decide to make these shoes in fabric). It is at this point where the decision of whether to make your shoes slings or pumps comes into play. If you're doing a pump follow the directions for drawing the top line of the shoe as demonstrated in chapter 5. If you are doing slings, use your pencil or Sharpie to draw the sling. For the bottom line, start at the arch of the foot and draw a graceful line (on both sides of the muslin) at an angle from the arch up to the rounded part of the heel. Next decide how high you want your vamp (and how wide you want your strap) to be. With these decisions in mind, draw a graceful line on both sides of the muslin from the vamp along the side of the foot (and above the line you drew from the arch) round the back to the top of the heel.

• Remove the muslin from the last, fold it in half, and true up and trim the pattern, so that each side of the muslin pattern is a mirror image of the other. Make them exactly the same. This is your "upper" pattern and we suggest that even though you are making leather shoes, that you mark the straight grain lines. Then should you decide to make fabric shoes out of this pattern you will have the straight grain lines already marked.

• Make the interlining pattern as outlined in chapter 5.

• The process for making the sole pattern is also the same as in the previous chapter. Trace the outline of your doll's foot on brown craft paper and cut it out.

• All the patterns, the "upper," the interlining, and the sole, should be traced onto card stock and then cut out. Remember to draw the straight grain lines on both the "upper" and interlining patterns.

• The "upper" and interlining pattern will always remain the same no matter which foot you are making the pattern for, but the sole is a different matter. The positioning of the sole is what determines the difference between the right and left foot. So when you are making shoes for a doll which has a definite right and left foot (as we are in this chapter), you are going to have to flip the pattern. We

Trimimng away the excess leather on the strap.

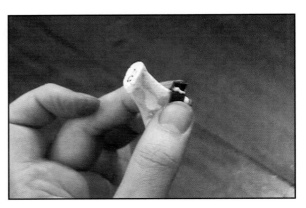

Glue is applied to the strap.

The strap is glued down.

Covering the heel with leather.

Trimming away the excess leather from the top of the heel.

The heel is ready to go on the shoe.

suggest marking one side R (this of course would be the side which corresponds to the right foot) and the opposite side L.

• The next step is to make the innersole, exactly as we did in the previous chapter. The only difference here is that for this pair of shoes we are going to use black acid free paper. The reason for this has to do with the difference between pumps and slings. With a pump the sole is completely covered, but with a sling the back section of the sole is exposed. And because the heel of these shoes is going to be black, we felt that if we used white acid free paper the color would "pop" against the black heel. So, we decided to use black paper to cut down on any possible discordant contrast.

• Lay the pattern for the shoe "upper" on the leather, and using an ultra fine point Sharpie trace the pattern onto the leather. You should be aware that Sharpies have the potential for bleeding through the leather so it will be to your advantage if you draw with a light hand.

• Lay the interlining pattern on the "upper" pattern you have just traced on the leather. Trace the lines of the interlining pattern onto the "upper" tracing on the leather.

• After you have traced the interlining pattern on the leather trace it onto a light-weight, tightly woven cotton and cut it out.

• Lay the interlining on the leather tracing, matching the lines, just as you did with the fusible in chapter 5, but instead of pressing with an iron, we are going to glue the cotton down on the leather. Brush the glue carefully onto the leather, taking care to stay within the interlining lines, and making sure the glue reaches the edge of the lines. Lay the cotton down, press it into place gently with your fingers and let it dry.

• Cut the leather tracing out, leaving a small seam allowance all around the entire tracing.

• Clip the inner curve (the top line of the shoe) to facilitate turning. Be careful with your clipping for you don't want clip marks to show on the finished side of the shoe.

• Lightly apply glue to the clipped section.

• Using your awl or any other pointed tool of your choice, turn the clipped edge

Coloring the raw edge of the innersole.

Applying glue to heel portion of the innersole.

Trimming the excess leather.

You can see there is a definite difference between the right and left foot.

back onto the cotton interlining.

• Use the backside of your awl (or a similar type tool) to press the clipped and turned edge down, thus making it nice and flat. Check the other side for irregularities or bumps. As the glue is still wet you can still lift the clips to re-arrange them or pull them tighter. Let the clipped edge dry thoroughly.

• The next step is to locate the point on your shoe where the upper section ends and the strap begins. Make a small diagonal cut into the corner, on both sides. (Refer to the picture if you are unsure as to where to cut.)

• Glue each strap section of the sling down onto the white cotton fabric. The bottom edge of each turned strap should be flush (no overhangs) at the end. If not, trim each strap end.

• It is at this point, when the leather shoe is still in a flat state, that if you want to decorate the toe area, this would be the time to do it.

• Next, you are going to attach the shoe to the innersole, just as we did with the fabric shoe in chapter 5. But here, instead of sewing, we are going to glue the stitch line to the innersole. We have found gluing to be preferable because we want a nice, soft, rounded toe, and if we sew the leather we will end up with a sharp point. Also, it is our experience that kid or any soft leather doesn't stand up to sewing well.

• Place your innersole on the last (leather side touching the last). Holding the innersole in place, dab a small amount of glue onto the toe point.

• Wrap your leather "upper" around the last, checking its position on the last as you do so. The edge of the interlining should come as close to the edge of the sole as you can get it. Your tracing lines will be an excellent guide to the placement of your "upper" on the last.

• Begin gluing the leather in place, stretching, pulling, and easing it as necessary. You may find it helps to use an awl or sharp tool to push and pull the leather and, achieve a good fit. You may also find it helps to clip away some of the excess leather as you go along. Keep pushing and working the leather until you get a smooth fit and a nice, rounded toe point.

• When you have your shoe to the place where you like the shape of it, rub the sole against a hard surface to help ensure that the sole is as flat as possible. This process is called burnishing and doing so also helps pull the leather tightly against the bottom of the last.

• Your next step will be to begin gluing along the arch of the shoe, where the edge of the interlining meets the edge of the innersole. Again, make sure the sole is as smooth as you can get it, because you don't want any bumps showing through the outer sole.

• Let the glue nearly dry, then pull the last out of your shoe to make sure the innersole is laying smoothly (hasn't buckled) and that none of the glue has adhered to the last.

• At this point you are going to glue the straps. Normally we would sew this section but, because the shoe is so small and the leather is fragile, it is our experience that gluing is the better option. The strap that is on the "outside" of the shoe is going to be brought round and glued on top of the "inside" strap of the shoe.

Trimming the excess leather off the outersole.

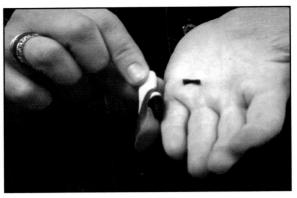

A decorative feature has been cut from black leather and will be glued to the back of the strap.

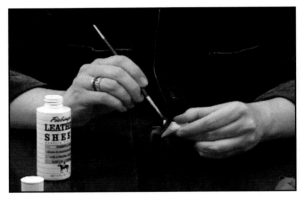

Applying the leather finish to the shoe.

The finished shoe.

• Begin by first pulling both straps to the back of the heel, checking to make sure that the fit on the last is snug and secure. If the straps are too long (which
sometimes happens because leather stretches) trim the excess away. Then bring the
"outside" strap round and overlap it over the "inside" strap.

• The overlap should not be more than 1/8 inch. Glue the overlap by placing a dab of glue on the "inside" strap, and laying the "outside strap on top of it. Let the glued strap dry completely.

• Cover the heel with leather, just as you covered the fabric heel in chapter 5. Leather doesn't have a bias so you don't have to worry about that, but leather does have enough of a natural stretch that it will hug your heel quite nicely.

• Because the heel is so small don't worry about folding the fabric over the bottom of it. Once the shank and the top edge of the heel is glued and covered, trim off any access leather on the bottom of the heel, flush with the bottom edge.

• Let the heel dry completely.

• Apply glue to the heel portion of the innersole.

• Place the heel on the shoe, making sure your orientation is straight. Using your fingers to apply pressure, hold the heel against the innersole until it is dry enough to let go.

• Use a pin or your fingernail to remove any glue that may have oozed out onto the shoe.

• In our sample shoe, it was at this point that we used a black indelible pen to color the raw edge of the innersole. Doing so gives the shoe just that much more of a finished look. But be careful when coloring, you don't want to get the ink on any other part of the shoe.

• Make the pattern for the outer sole and cut it out of leather, just as was done in chapter 5. One thing you will discover is that because the shoe is so small, the breast of the heel part of the pattern will be much narrower than it was for the Cissy shoe. Make sure you match the left outer sole with left shoe and vice-versa.

• Paint the suede side of the outer sole with glue and apply it to the shoe. Using your awl and other tools, press the breast section as well as the rest of the sole into place.

• Trim any excess leather off the sole. Try to do each side with one sweep of the scissors to prevent jagged edges.

• Using a leather punch, punch out a circle for the lift. Use a pin to pick the circle out of the punch. Paint the bottom of the heel (the lift section) with glue. Place the leather circle (suede side on the glue) on the bottom of the heel. Clean up any excess glue.

• Let the shoe dry completely.

• If you plan on adding any pieces of cutout leather to the shoe as a decorative touch (see chapter 7), do so now.

• *Apply a leather finish (following package instructions) to the entire exterior of the shoe, if you so desire. The leather finish gives a nice gloss to the shoe, as well as covering any imperfections in the leather. Apply 1 or 2 coats (your choice), let the finish dry, then buff the shoe. If you do choose do to more than one coat, let the finish dry completely before applying a second coat. The down side of using a leather finish is that it will change the color of the leather by darkening it. We like the finished look it gives the shoe and the fact that it also protects the leather, so we accommodate for the change in color when choosing our leather. But if you would prefer an alternative, use a shoe wax, apply it lightly according to package instructions, and buff it after the wax has dried.*

• *Make your second leather shoe.*

The finished sling back shoe made for Ashton Drake's Gene.

Hints & Tips

Before putting your shoes on your doll, you might want to stuff the toe point with cotton. Because the doll's foot will not go to the tip of the shoe, the cotton insertion will prevent the toe box from collapsing, as well as help keep the shoe snugly on your doll's foot.

When making the lift for a very small shoe, it helps to use a leather punch rather than trying to cut it out freehand. Using the punch will give you a perfectly shaped lift.

Remember, when choosing a leather for the "upper" part of your doll shoe, kid works best. Its soft pliability makes it an ideal leather when working with miniature shapes. A wonderful source for kid is old gloves which can be found at flea markets and secondhand shops. Just make sure, before purchasing gloves that they are still "viable". You can test the leather by pulling the gloves gently. If they crack, shred, or tear, look for another pair.

When applying leather finish or wax to your completed shoes, do so lightly. Too heavy a hand could ruin the look of your new shoes.

Be careful, when working with steps that involve gluing, not to get any glue on the outside surface of your shoe. This is important, because when you apply the leather finish or wax, any glue spots will show up as a mar on the leather.

Ribbons, beads and trims all add perfect "finishing touches".

Chapter 7

<u>Finishing Touches</u>

You now have at least one pair of beautifully made shoes, and the question before you is, do you like the shoes just as they are or do you want to embellish them with trim or decoration? It may just be that additional decoration is superfluous and somewhat over the top. There is something to be said about the time-honored maxim of less being more. The fabric you have chosen or the gloss of the leather may be all the shoe needs. It is a matter of taste and what suits you, and, the outfit the shoes will accessorize. However, should you feel that your shoes need an extra something to give them a more "finished" look, there are any number of things you can do to give them just a bit of " je ne sais quoi". Ribbons tied into small bows and glued onto your shoes, on the toe box or at the back of the heel certainly look chic, and small flowers always add a pretty touch.

But these are not the only options available to you. In fact, looking for imaginative decorative touches for your shoes can be a source of great fun, for it can lead to a treasure hunt. Trips to flea markets and antique stores as well an any other source you can think of, may reward you with finds of tiny silver buckles, "diamond" or "cut steel" circles or, better yet, little treasures you never thought of until you started looking. Keep an eye out, as you go about your daily life, for wonderful, unusual buttons, and beautiful beads to sew on, at the toe area. You may be surprised at what you can find in the most unlikely places that can be adapted to enhancing a shoe. Just remember that whatever you think of or plan to do, it must be in scale with the size of your shoe.

Scale, which is a matter of proportion and size, is often a problem for manufacturers as well as doll lovers and artists. The realistic model upon which all dolls and every aspect of their clothing and accessories are based is, of course, the human one. The adaptation of human size to a realistic miniature can be very difficult, for the results have to be such that they look right to the eye. Small or even tiny objects which look "real" as well as having the correct proportional size or scale, can be very hard to come by. Often, a millimeter can make the difference between a piece of trim or a decoration that is the right size and one that looks a little out of whack. It is hard to tell sometimes. Should that be the case and you find you have doubts about a pending choice, our advice is, don't use the item in question. Your "eye" is warning you that something may not be quite right and you would be wise to heed it.

This will also be true should you choose to embroider your fabric shoe, or decorate the leather shoe with cutout pieces of leather. Take care that your embroidery or beading pattern, the size of the beads, as well as any leather cutouts, compliments the size of the shoe rather than overwhelming it. And, as we suggested in chapters 5 and 6, if you are going to add a decoration to the toe box, do it while the shoe is still in a flat shape, before you put it on the last. It will be so much easier to do your hand work while the shoe is in this stage rather than trying to accomplish it once it has assumed it's shoe shape. We also suggest that you work out any embroidery or beading designs on paper first. This, as you may guess, will help eliminate the possibility of mistakes before attempting to do it directly on the shoe, where, once done, the work is irreversible.

Our favorite way of decorating leather shoes is, as we mentioned, to cut interesting shapes out of a different color leather and glue them onto the shoe. We did that in chapter 6, when a small black leather bow was glued on the back of the heel to camouflage the seam. A more elaborate scheme of decoration is pictured here, in this chapter. Pink leather cutouts were glued onto green shoes. The toe box was decorated before the "upper" was glued to the last, and the remaining trim was put on after the shoes were completed but before the liquid finish was painted on. And, once the shoes were dry, we placed them in their own little shoe box.

Yes that's right, shoe boxes, another aspect of finishing touches. What better way to store your beautifully designed shoes, or present a pair to a friend, as a gift, than in a custom made box? After you've gone to all the trouble of making such lovely shoes, it is only fitting that they should have their own box. We give you, here in this chapter, a pattern for shoe boxes. One that will fit the shoes made in chapter 6. If you adapt the techniques and pattern in this book to make even larger shoes, do the same with the boxes. Go to your local copy center and have them enlarge the pattern. Along with the box we also provide you with a design for the outside. Use ours or design your own.

So, now you have shoes and you have boxes. "What's next," you may be asking, and our answer is, "that's up to you." You have the techniques, you have the imagination, and now the sky is the limit. You can make your classic pumps and heels, and no doubt you will, for after all, that is the main thrust of this book. But there are other avenues that could be explored. You might include a bit of whimsy in your shoemaking plans.

A pair of bunny slippers like the ones pictured in this chapter, were fun to make and gave a great deal of pleasure to the recipient. Or try your hand at a pair of more definitive period shoes, like those from the cavalier period, and then design an outfit, ala three musketeers for example, to go with them.

You can also, once you have several pairs of beautiful shoes, do as we have done, and create personalized stationery and notecards, for sale or for your own private use. These paper goods would be a wonderful alternative way of showcasing the shoes you have just made. Why not show off your creations, and the skill you acquired to make them, in such an absolutely unique way? You deserve credit for the work you've done.

The point is, and the one we would like to make here, is that just the fact that you purchased this book tells us a great deal about you. It is clear to us that you are a perfectionist and a seeker of beauty. If you weren't, you would be content with the plastic or ribbon shoes so many manufacturer's offer with the dolls they sell. But you're not, and like us, you want all the details to be just right. You are willing to spend time and money towards achieving that end. And now that you have the skills that will enable you to satisfy your desire for perfection, we say go for it. Take what you've learned here and make it your own. But don't stop there, experiment and expand your knowledge. We wish you the best and are confident that you'll soon become known as someone who is an expert at making beautiful doll shoes.

Use your shoes for inspiration, as we have done here. A selection of Tim's shoes become a lovely heading for a set of personal stationery.

Exclusive Tim Alberts Shopping Bag

A

B

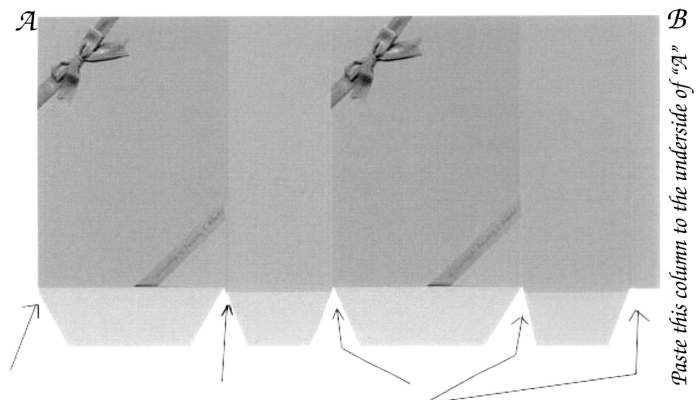

Paste this column to the underside of "A"

Fold here, and score along the lines

cut

cut

Shoe box design coordinates with shopping bag

To Make the Shopping Bag

· Score along the lines that signify the front and back of the shopping bag, as designated by the bow decorations.

· Score along the entire bottom gently, but don't cut.

· Fold in the four bottom panels, small side panels first.

· Glue the bottom panels together with a small dab of Sobo glue.

· Choose a thin cord or ribbon for each handle. The ribbon should be 3" long.

· Using white paper tape, cut a piece of tape to line the top inside of the bag.

· Line up your handle in the center, making sure there is enough height for the doll's hand to go through.

· Tape the ribbon or cord to the inside of the bag.

Making the Shoe Box

· The shoe box is shaded in three colors for you to follow the cuts and places to score.

· The top of the box has the bow design on it. Make small cut marks from the outside of each cut mark to the tip of the box top design.

· Lightly score around the box top, to delineate where the folds go.

· Bend down all four sides.

· Bend the hanging edges of the top pieces inward.

· Fold the gray panels underneath the lilac.

· Place a tiny dab of Sobo glue on the hanging edges.

· Insert the hanging edge of the top piece into the folded gray panel.

· Let dry.

· With the bottom of the box, lightly score around the dark lilac bottom of the box.

· Fold all four flaps upward.

· Score along the darker lines of the end panels.

· Glue the flaps to the inside of the box.

Now you have an exclusive Timothy J. Alberts shoe box and shopping bag!

Elise, a 19th century "Smiling" Bru is dressed in the clothing of the day, with matching leather pumps. Designed by Timothy J. Alberts. From the collection of Doug James.

Visual Shoe Dictionary

BOOTS

Despite pre-historic evidence, with the exception of riding boots, boots were primarily worn by men. Women's riding boots were, and remain to this day, a scaled down version of the men's boot.

In other cultures women wore boots as part of their everyday dress. These were a soft sock type of footwear similar to those nomadic women wore when traversing desert sands.

Chinese women of the privileged class wore soft boots called "lotus boots" which were designed to cover the 3-inch bound foot which was so valued in Chinese society.

In the 1750s, while shoes remained low cut, women began to wear a laced up riding boot which extended above the ankle.

In the 1830s and 1840s ankle high boots, with elastic sides, or invisible laces at the ankle, were adapted for everyday wear. These were massed produced in the 1850s thus making them available to all women.

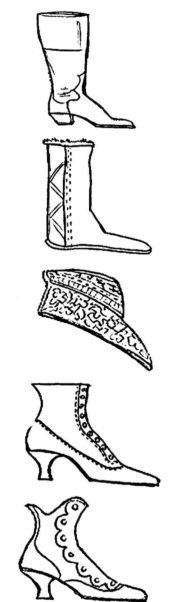

In the 1860s, lace-up the front boots were introduced.

The gay 90s produced the elaborate and highly decorated opera boots.

Low or pants boot were popular in the late 1950s and 60s.

The Go-Go boot of the 1960s created a fashion craze along with their thigh high counterpart which looked very similiar to the cavalier boots worn from 1625-1660.

In the 1970s, the laced up boot which extended up the calf, and had first made it's appearance in 1885, was re-discovered.

Boots worn in the late 1970s, then again the 1990s looked very much like the opera boots of the1890s.

Galoshes, which more than make up for their dull appearance by providing excellent protection for the feet against the elements, are an adaptation of a shoe once worn by the Gauls.

Wellies are named for the Duke Of Wellington and are a close version of the the boots he wore during his many military campaigns at the end of the 1790s and the beginning of the 19th century, notably at Waterloo.

Gaiters, from the middle of the 18th century through the first part of the 20th century, served a dual purpose. First, as a protector of shoes from inclement weather, and secondly, as the means of making a shoe look like a boot. Buttoned on the side, they were usually made from leather or linen.

High Heels

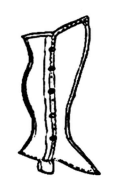

Like hemlines, heels on shoes have fallen or risen according to the whims and dictates of fashion. They made their first real appearance and subsequent fashion statement during the Elizabethan era. But the heels of that time were slight, made from cork, and would hardly cause a blip on today's fashion radar screen.

Historical gossip reports that Catherine de Medici, a woman short in stature if not power, wore heels to her wedding with the Duc d'Orleans, the future King Henry II of France, though truth be told, the heels she wore were most probably a pair of elevated shoes rather than "heels" as we have come to know them.

From 1660 until after the French revolution in 1789, shoes had heels.

Marie Antoinette wore a pair of heeled shoes, a la Turque, in the early 1790s.

In the 1830s, after disappearing for well over a quarter century, heels returned from obscurity and took over the shoe fashion scene, never to disappear again.

It was in the 1950s, right along side Dior's New Look, that the heeled shoe became the "High Heel," a foot sensation.

Designers, wild with possibility, created the ultimate high heel, the stiletto. So high were these heels, often over four inches, that a steel rod was inserted into the heel itself to stabilize the structure and add strength to the shoe.

High heels have maintained their own through the 1970s, when platforms were so favored, the 1980s and, the1990s. There is such a variety of designs available that it is now simply a matter of choosing to suit your taste, and foot.

Platforms

Platforms would fit quite easily into the "everything old is new again" category. When they first appeared on the feet of sons and daughters at the end of the 1960s and into the 1970s, parents were aghast that their children would want to place such "oddities" upon their feet.

In fact, people have been wearing platforms in one form or another since history began. Plain wooden clogs, which exist to this very time, were used by early European peasants to protect their feet while they worked their farms.

During the Renaissance, the wealthy wore clogs as protectors for their finely made, valuable shoes.

Chopines, popular in Venice during the Renaissance, and originally Turkish in origin, were basically slippers on a platform. The idea was to place your shod foot into the slipper and thus be able to walk the watery streets of Venice without getting your feet wet. The problem with Chopines was that many of them were so high, up to 30 inches, that one couldn't walk without teetering. This made the need of at least one escort, but preferably two, mandatory.

Pattens ducked in and out of fashion history from the 14th to the end of the 18th century. These not very stylish shoe protectors were wooden soles attached to a pedestal or platform. The shoe was held to the patten by wide leather bands.

European women weren't alone in their use of platforms. Japanese women have worn Getas for centuries. These "sandal" platforms are generally designed as a simple wooden "shoe," but for formal occasions elaborate or decorated Getas are available.

Both Korean and Chinese women had shoes, which were either a variation of the clog or the wooden platform, in their closets.

At the end of the 1930s and heading into the 1940s, movie stars such as Joan Crawford and Betty Grable influenced fashion, principally shoe fashion, by wearing platforms in their films. Credit must also be given to the designers who dressed the stars and, most notably, to Carmen Miranda, the tiny star, who almost single-handedly created the trend.

With the sleek appeal of Dior's "New Look," platforms disappeared, not to appear again for 20 years, in the1970s, and then 20 years after that, in the 1990s.

PUMPS

Pumps are enclosed shoes. They have gone through a myriad of incarnations since they first came on the scene, nearly 500 years ago, but the bottom line on pumps is that they are enclosed shoes.

The first time the word "pumps" appears in writing, referring to shoes, is during the reign of Elizabeth I. Those first pumps were a low-cut shoe, or slipper, with an upper made from leather or velvet that could be decorated or embroidered. The heels on most of these shoes were slight and made of cork.

By the time of Charles I (1625-1660) the pump had acquired a long vamp, a high tongue, a toe that was rounded at the tip, and high square heels. The shoe was open at the sides and fastened at the instep with ribbon ties called latchets.

By the end of the 17th century, the pump was beginning to look more like the pump of the 20th century. It had lost the long tongue and the open sides, giving the pump a more enclosed look. Heels, though still on the high side, varied according to taste.

The beginning of the 18th century brought with it pointed toes and the French or "Louis" heel..

The shoes of the second half of the 18th century remained similar to those of the first half of that century but became more elegant and refined, due presumably to the exquisite taste of Marie Antoinette.

As the Regency period in England (First Empire in France), progressed into the Victorian era, the pump began to acquire a heel.

By the 1870s the pump was fully heeled and looked like a simpler version of the 18th century shoe.

From the 1870s until the 1950s, variations of this shoe, with straps, without, with tongues and buckles, or without, made in leathers and beautiful fabrics graced the feet of the world's women.

In the 1950s, a hallmark era as far as fashion is concerned, Hubert de Givenchy re-thought the pump, refined it, restored it's bare essence, and presented the world with an enduring classic.

In the years following the 1950s, whether the pump has stayed in the forefront of the shoe scene, or slipped into the background, it has stayed a classic.

Sandals

At their most basic, sandals are the shape of the sole cut from a sturdy material and were held to the foot by strips of leather, fabric, or rope.

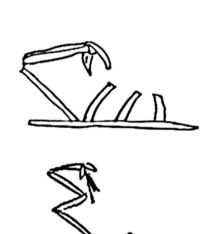

The Egyptians and the wandering tribes of Judea wore them, as did the the Romans, who called them calcei. There are very few societies who have not, if any, worn sandals.

As fashion progressed into the 20th century sandals acquired sophistication, exotic & exciting shapes, embellishments, and heels.

Their influence has been seen everywhere, from Japanese Getas, to sporty, sensible shoes, to the strappy high heels seen in the fashion magazines.

"Sensible Shoes"

Aside from being shoes your mother always advised you to wear, sensible shoes are otherwise known as sport or walking shoes. Traditionally these shoes have first been made for men and then adapted for women.

The oxford which have been worn by men since around 1885, began to be worn by women during WWI Black, brown or russet leather are the colors for fall and winter, white buckskin for summer.

Brogues are a sturdier oxford. This lace-up shoe follows the same summer/winter color scheme the oxford does. And, as with the oxford, women began to adopt these oh so comfortable shoes with the advent of WWI.

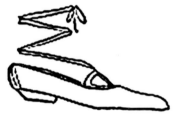

Gillies (or Ghillies) are an adaption of a "shoe" worn by old Germanic tribes. Originally, these were a piece of leather wrapped around the foot and tied around the ankle with leather thongs.Today these brown leather shoes are still popular in Scotland and Ireland.

Saddle shoes, worn by millions of school children, are white buckskin with either a brown or black saddle (the instep).

Today's sensible shoes, fulfill the need of the modern woman to walk, run, and race through their lives, and still look good, or at the very least fashionable.

Slippers

Slippers are the chameleons of the shoe world. Trimmed with marabou or other frothy confections they can be as intimate and sexy as a boudoir "shoe" ought to be. Make it out of silk faille, trim it with a bow or glittering rhinestones, and it is ready for a night on the town.

The Turkish slipper which traveled to Europe, from it's mother country, in the company of the crusaders, has inspired shoe design right through the 20th century.

The Turkish influence can also be seen in the pixie boots of the 1960s.

Mules, in their simplest form are backless shoes. They first showed up in Europe, during Elizabethan times. Then, as they do now, they served a dual purpose. As pantofles they served as shoe coverings. As mules they were bedroom slippers, much as they can be today.

In the 1800s, it should be remembered, all delicate or fragile footwear were called slippers. At the same time there was an actual style of shoe that was given the name "slipper."

The slipper worn in Regency England and Bonapartist France, was a delicate affair made from tissue thin kid or fabric, low, or no, heeled.

From the beginning of the 19th century to 1820 the slipper toe had a tapered round shape. Or after that, around the beginning the 1830s, the toe was squared off. Then, throughout the rest of the Victorian era, you could find, rounded, tapered round, or squared off toes, depending upon on one's taste.

In 1860, heels were added to the flat version of the slipper, thus making it more like a pump.

The slipper, or flat shoe, may have gone out of fashion in Victorian England but it came back in modern times in the form of ballet shoes, and as flats such as the Capezio's that were so popular in the 1950s and 1960s or as low-heeled shoes worn for day or evening in the 1980s and 1990s.

The ever popular bedroom slipper.

Shoes don't grow on trees, except for this special Topiary,
designed by Timothy J. Alberts.

Glossary

Alginate ..... *A casting compound used primarily by dentists, taxidermists, and professional make-up artists.*

Awl ..... *A "small pointed tool used for piercing holes" in fabric, leather, and paper. Can be found hardware or artist supply stores.*

Bias ...... *When you cut on the bias the grain line is moved to a position that is, at its most, a 45 degree angle from the selvedge edge. Bias provides stretch and give. When making shoes, it is advantageous to use bias when covering the heels, because the bias will hug the round shapes, thus making it easier to cover the heels smoothly.*

Breast ..... *The breast is the forward-front section of the heel.*

Burnish .....*To burnish means to make something smooth. In this book, the soles are made smooth by rubbing them against a hard surface.*

Calipers ..... *A "two-legged" measuring instrument available at stationery, artist supply or hardware stores.*

Curing ..... *The process of allowing something (such as a mold) to dry completely.*

Dremel ..... A small drilling machine which has an assortment of and bits. The drum sander attachment is a wonderful aid when sanding the wooden last.

Fashion Toe ..... The extension beyond the toe line which defines the fashion toe of the time or the style of the shoe you are making.

Finger Pressing...... This is when you use a finger/nail, to open and flatten a seam.

Fusible ..... Fusible, in this book, refers to iron-on interlining. It is coated with a glue on one side, and when you lay fusible on a fabric and apply heat, the interlining will bond or fuse with the surface it has been applied to.

Grain Line ..... A straight line which determines the straight grain of fabric.

Heel ..... The bottom-back part of the shoe which provides height and support.

Innersole ..... The inner part of the shoe upon which the foot rests.

Instep ..... The instep is the bottom of the arch

Last ..... An exact replica of the foot and the solid shape upon which a shoe is built.

Leather Finish ..... A liquid which, when applied to a finished shoe, softens the leather and supplies a patina. Fiebing's leather sheen was used on the doll shoes featured in this book.

Lift ..... The lift is the bottom-most section of the heel. It serves the dual purpose of finishing off the heel while at the same time protecting the bottom of the heel with contact with the ground.

Liquid Rubber Latex ..... A brush on liquid rubber used to make molds.

Mold ..... A hollow form used to give a solid shape to something which is in a liquid or molten form.

Mold (To) ..... *A technique used to shape a solid, or change the shape of one solid into an alternative or different shape.*

Profile ..... *An outline or silhouette of a shape or solid.*

Quarter ..... *The quarter is located at the back part of the shoe and fits the sides of the heel.*

Sharpie ..... *A fine point permanent marker found in stationery stores.*

Selvage Edge ..... *The edge of a piece of cloth. On most (if not all) fabrics, this edge is so woven as to not unravel, nor does it need a hem. Its appearance is of a smooth line running down the sides of the fabric, regardless of the fabric itself.*

Slurry ..... *A "thin mixture of water and an insoluble material" such alginate, plaster of Paris, or water putty.*

Sole ..... *Also called the outer sole, the sole is the bottom of the shoe.*

Throat ..... *The throat is the top line of the shoe, that which start at the vamp and fits around the foot.*

Toe Box ..... *Is at the front of the shoe and is where the toes fit. The size and shape of the toe box is determined by a combination of the size and shape of the toes and the fashion toe extension.*

"Truing Up" a Pattern ..... *Technically speaking, "truing is the process of connecting all points on a pattern and checking for accuracy of measurement." Here, in this book, it refers specifically to the process of straightening and refining (with the use of straight rulers and curves) lines transferred from the muslin patterns.*

"Upper" ..... *In this book the term upper or "upper" refers to the upper part of the shoe, that which sits on top of the foot as opposed to the sole which is always under the foot.*

Vamp ..... *The vamp of the shoe covers the arch section of the foot. In period or sporty shoes, the vamp is where the tongue is situated.*

Paris, a doll made by Timothy J. Alberts, guides us through the resources needed to make your own wonderful shoes!

Source Guide

The materials used in this book, and for which sources are provided here, are the ones we use and have found to be most effective for making our doll shoes. However, as you become familiar with the techniques, you may find other products which you prefer and, which work just as well. Use them! After all, experimentation is an important part of the creative process and and the sources listed here are only suggestions.

Alginate: This casting compound can be found in many artist supply stores. If you cannot find it in your town, you can order it from : Van Dyke's, Woodsocket, South Dakota 1-800-843-3320

When ordering alginate, be aware that some alginates are "quick set." Because the nature of the product is to set up very quickly, you want to give yourself a time advantage by purchasing standard alginate. Also, keep in mind that to make molds as described in chapters 2 and 4, the slurry (or mix) must be pourable. This may mean adding more water than the manufacturer suggests. Consequently, it may take your mold a little longer to set up than the package says. It would be best if you experiment with the alginate, trying it out a few times, before actually making your molds.

Durham's Water Putty: You should be able to find this product at your local hardware store. If not, you can contact the company directly and ask them for the name of a local supplier.

The Donald Durham Company
Des Moines, Iowa
(515) 243-0491

Leather: A good source for soft leather for uppers (only) is old kid gloves. These can be found at flea markets or secondhand stores. You will also need a leather source for the lightweight-medium leather. You can also look in the yellow pages to see if there are any leather supply stores in your town. If there are none, you can order from Van Dyke's (listed above, under alginate), but we caution you, that when speaking with a rep, they may suggest a packet of pigskin scraps that they sell. But the holes left in the skin after the removal of the bristles, make pigskin unattractive for doll use. They have a wide range of leathers at Van Dyke's, so you should have no problems finding a leather to suit your needs.

Another source for leather is the Leather Factory. They have an enormous stock of leathers and are able to supply any leather you may choose or need.

The Leather Factory
1818 N. Cameron Street
Harrisburg, Pennsylvania 17110
1-800-233-7155

Leather Finish: A leather finish applied to a completed shoe, softens shoe and adds a lovely patina to the leather. If you prefer not to use a leather finish, you can wax and buff the shoe to achieve the desired patina. If you do choose a leather finish, it is best to check local shoe repair stores to see what products they stock. For the shoes in this book, we have used "Fiebing's Leather Sheen". Fiebing products can be found at most shoe repair shops. If you cannot find them, you contact the company directly.

Fiebing's
516 South 2nd Street
Milwaukee, Wisconsin 53204
(414) 271-3769

Liquid Rubber Latex: We use a liquid rubber latex that sells under the brand name of "Mold Builder". This can be found at artist supply stores. If you cannot find it, you can get in touch with the manufacturer directly and ask them for a source near you. "Mold Builder" is sold by:

ETI
Field's Landing, California
(707) 443-9323

Marking –Pencil Removal: Look for this product in you local notions sewing store. If you cannot find it, we suggest you contact the manufacturer directly.

Quilter's Rule Int'l Inc.
2322 N.E. 29th Ave.
Ocala, Fla. 34470
1-352-368-9048

Ribbon: Most towns and cities have sources for ribbons. You can find them in fabric and trim shops. And, doll and craft magazines an abundance of adds for sources of ribbon. An excellent source for ribbons and trims that we can suggest is:

Sandy's Victorian Trims
7417 N. Knoxville
Peoria, Ill. 61614
(309) 689-1943

Sobo Glue: Although there are many good glues, Sobo is the one we prefer. It does exactly what we wish without leaking through, thus marring the fabric or leather of your shoe. We have also found, though we do not know how or why it happens, that Sobo has a tendency to soften leather make it more pliable. You should be able to find this at stationery or artist supply stores. If not, you can contact the manufacturer directly and ask for the location of a supplier near you. Sobo is made by:

Delta Technical Coatings
2550 Pellissier Place
Whittier, Calif. 90601
1-800-423-4135

Trims: Finding trims, such as flowers, buckles and other decorations is always difficult because of the small scale required for dolls. We always keep our eyes peeled when at flea markets, antiquing, looking in magazines, and craft stores. Many areas are lucky enough to have huge craft stores such as "Michael's." If you have access to such stores, check them out, for you never know what you will find where, and unexpected finds are such a pleasure. It also helps if you have a definite source for trims, and we have one we would like to include in our source guide. These ladies even make flowers!

Tinsel Trading Company
47 West 38th St.
New York, N.Y. 10018
(212) 730-1030

*Ashton Drake's Gene®, weary after a day of trying
to find shoes that look great and fit well!
Coat, dress, hat and shoes designed exclusively by Timothy J. Alberts.*

Patterns

The patterns shown here are the ones used to create the fabric shoes in chapter 5 and the leather shoes in chapter 6. You'll notice that the sole pattern for the fabric shoes is a universal pattern, meaning, as you now know, that it can be used for both the right and left foot. The sole pattern for the leather shoe will have to be flipped, as we described in chapter 6, to accommodate the difference between the right and left foot. You can also see the difference between the shape of the pattern for the pump as compared to that of the sling.

These patterns can be copied and used, as a shortcut, rather than draping your own pattern, but you will still need the last to successfully make your shoes. And these patterns will only serve you well if the shoes being made are for dolls that have the same size and shape foot as the dolls the patterns were made for.

Pattern for Cissy Shoe
(Universal Foot)

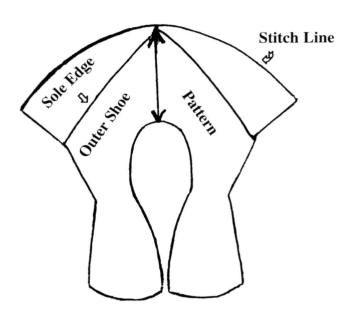

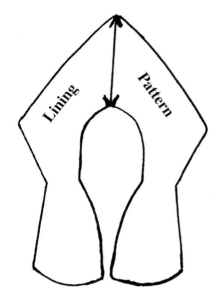

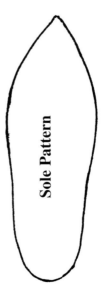

Profile for Carved Last
as demonstrated in Chapter 3

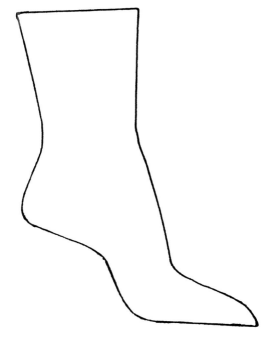

UNIVERSAL SOLE PATTERN

Pattern is actual size for Cissy Wedding Shoe described in Chapter 5.

Sling Pattern for Gene®
as demonstrated in Chapter 6

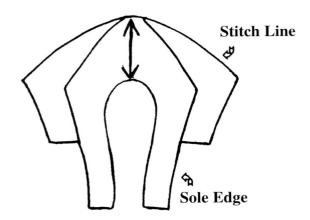

Stitch Line

Sole Edge

Outer Shoe Pattern with Placement for Lining

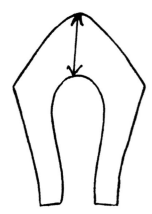

Lining Pattern

Pay special attention to the straight ↕ grain lines

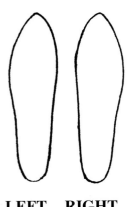

LEFT   RIGHT
Innersole Pattern

Gene®
Shoe
Sole
Pattern

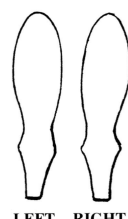

LEFT   RIGHT
Outersole Pattern

106

Pump Pattern for Gene®

Stitch Line

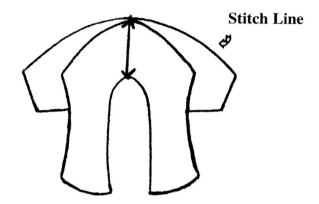

Outer Shoe Pattern with Placement for Lining

Lining Pattern

NOTE: Pay special attention to the straight ⬍ grain lines

What could be sweeter?

Acknowledgements

We'd like to thank all the family members and friends who offered us their support. In particular we'd like to thank Sonia Rivera of the Fashion Doll Scene, for not only suggesting that we turn what was once only a video into a book, but for her continuing support and help. We also extend our gratitude to Hal Aronow-Theil for allowing us to spend so many hours in his photography studio/dining room, and, for converting shots from the video into stills. And, we are most appreciative that Doug James allowed us to photograph his 19th century Smiling Bru doll, Elise, and include her in our book.

About the Authors

Timothy J. Alberts is a renown doll creator and designer. He is currently best known for his design work on the Gene doll. He is also a successful costume supervisor for films, such as "Sabrina," "The Devil's Own," the current "Random Hearts," and "What Lies Beneath," starring Harrison Ford and Michelle Pfeiffer. He also has several new fashion doll projects which will make their appearance in 2000 and 2001.

M. Dalton King is the business partner of Timothy J. Alberts and the author of such books as "Special Teas" and "Perfect Preserves."

Pat Henry is a fashion stylist in New York, and writer for fashion doll publications such as The Fashion Doll Scene, and Barbie Bazaar. She is also the designer of "Patpaks," miniature props and accessories for fashion dolls. This is her first collaboration on a book, as photographer, illustrator and art director.

Coming soon - our next book, "The Art of Miniature Millinery".

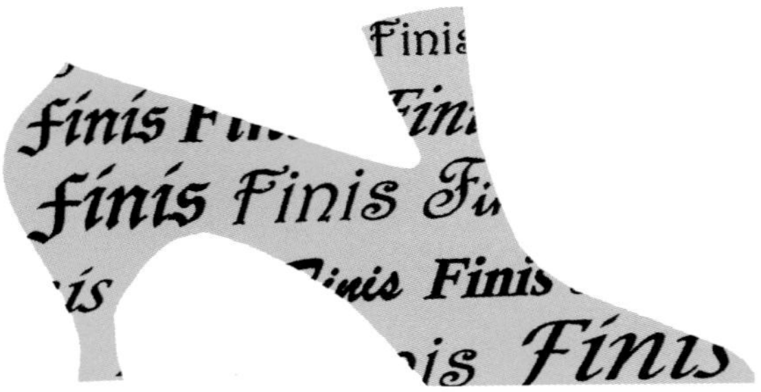
Finis
finis
finis Finis
Finis

PML

25